MW01142982

This book made m
shows the extreme ?
raised in Canada do
perity we have which they take for granted.
—*Dorothy Babin*

This book is a "real life" thriller!
It was my honoured privilege to be Lidia Pater's pastor when she first arrived in Canada. The first time she publicly shared some of this exciting account was in our church, I believe. I remember too, how earlier with strong conviction, John, the husband who had abandoned her, confessed to me the change that had come into his life through Jesus Christ and his determination to be reunited with his wife. This book relates Lidia's struggles with loneliness and the questioning of her returning husband's sincerity. This is an exciting read. You will follow her as she walks for days through mountain forests, and crosses the mighty Danube river at night, though unable to swim. All in her effort to escape a Communist stronghold and to re-establish a home with her "new" former husband. The unseen hand of God is shown to be visibly involved!
—*Pastor Elmer S. Martin*

For years I've been heckling my mom to write a book about her life. There have been many, many occasions that a conversation segues into the topic of my Romanian heritage and how my family came to Canada. Before my mom wrote her story I would cringe at the thought of my unjust retelling of my mom's incredible adventure. There simply isn't enough time in a brief conversation to encapsulate the miracle of my parent's reconciliation after 14 years of bitter separation. This book is a testament to the greatness of our God, who brought two people back together against incredible odds. I am so proud of you mom!
—*Becky Pater*

Dear L.C.R.C. Maranatha
staff & members, thank you for

LIDIA PATER

returning the document to me.
I appreciate that. May God richly
bless you all & your families

Ps. 66 : 16 - 20

Praying
FOR MY

NEXT

My Prayerful Journey Back to My Ex

Feb 9, 2016

ISBN:978-1-77069-593-1

Printed in Canada

Word Alive Press
131 Cordite Road, Winnipeg, MB R3W 1S1
www.wordalivepress.ca

Library and Archives Canada Cataloguing in Publication
Pater, Lidia, 1952-
        Praying for my next / Lidia Pater.
ISBN 978-1-77069-593-1

        1. Marriage. 2. Married people. I. Title.
HQ134.P38 2012   306.8   C2012-903103-8

dedication

This book is gratefully dedicated to the memory of my mother, who stood by me when times were tough. She fasted with me all the Tuesdays of one year, and many other days, and did everything she could to help her children. When she died, we were all married and had families. Thank God for godly mothers!

table of contents

acknowledgements

I want to express a heartfelt thank you to several people who helped and supported me in writing this book.

First of all, I owe a big thank you to my family, who was very understanding and cheered me on: John, my husband, who really loves me, and our children, Sam and Becky, who were also excited about the book. I want to say a very special thank you to Becky, who was diligent, knowledgeable, and eager to edit the first draft of my writing.

To Evan Braun, the editor from Word Alive Press, I want to express my gratitude for bringing a clearer meaning to the words and phrases in my story.

Last but not least, a warm thank you to Tiffany Trithardt from Word Alive Press for her many kind words, good suggestions, and excellent ideas.

May God richly bless you all.

OR VICTIM?

1

We were two hundred metres from the Danube. The vegetation was lush and green, but the leaves under our feet were dry and crackly. It was eleven o'clock at night and so dark that I couldn't see my hand in front of my face.

Suddenly, two huge dogs came at us, barking fiercely, ready to rip us apart. We froze. I could feel the breath of the bigger dog on me. Its foamy saliva and white fangs glistened in the pitch dark night. Its deep, angry growls seemed to fill my whole universe. All the hair on my body stood up. We didn't dare move. We were petrified.

Those dry leaves could betray our presence. If we moved an inch, it would crack the whole world. A soldier could be behind those dogs, pointing his rifle at us. Perhaps a local shepherd would follow his dogs and see us at the end of his flashlight's beam.

The dogs kept threatening us. We became statues and stopped breathing. As our last meal together, we'd shared some salami with bread and half an apple each. Most likely, the dogs had smelled the salami and chased after us.

We were so close to freedom! But jail or death were just as close. We prayed desperately.

Lord, please, help us!

Was it worth it to risk our lives to get out of Romania? There was no turning back now. We had to press on. We were growing numb, yet we kept praying, praying, praying...

Lord!

Help!

Please, help us!

Our silent prayers went up. Was this the end? I had thought it was just the beginning.

What am I doing? Where am I going? Will I get out of this alive? Is this really worth the risk I'm taking, trying to follow my ex-husband out of this iron curtain country? Who is this man I'm going with? Can I trust him? How do I know if he'll be true to me?

Very few women took this path. Usually the men escaped and their families followed. In my case, that had been impossible. I had waited so many years. How had it all started?

THE MOST *Beloved* SON OF THE PEOPLE

2

The Romania I grew up in was communist. I was born in December 1952 in Arad, a big city of about 180,000 people in the western part of the country. Russia was the powerful neighbour on the eastern side of the border. My city was twenty-five kilometres away from the Hungarian border. Between Hungary and Germany was Austria, a beautiful little country. I'd grown up with a Western influence.

Having lived in Canada for twenty-five years, I realize that it's hard to imagine life under an oppressive regime. Every business and company was government-owned. There wasn't a single private business in a country of twenty-two million people. Not one. There were huge industrial companies that employed up to twenty thousand people. Everybody had a job. There were no beggars on the streets.

Nicolae Ceausescu became leader of the council in 1965, and in 1974 he became the President of Romania. You might say that he started out good, but in time he became very corrupt. Every August, there were huge crowds of people parading in front of the political officials seated in the centre of each city, praising the "freedom of the people" from the capitalist regime.

Every so often, Ceausescu would visit parts of the country. People had to stop working and were driven out into the streets like sheep, waiting hours for the "most beloved son of the people" to pass by in his car with a huge entourage of motorcycles and security cars following. People had to wave and cheer loudly. Occasionally, he would visit factories. The workers had to shine and polish everything.

His comments were received with great accolades. Whether Ceausescu visited a bakery, a smelting furnace, or a chicken complex, he always told people how to do their jobs better. He had no business expertise; he was just exerting his power. All of those recommendations were called "comrade Ceausescu's precious indications" by the media.

A lot of informers were hired as security. You couldn't make a single negative comment about the President, for you never knew who would turn you in. You could be either thrown in jail for many years or killed.

At some point, Ceausescu decided to pay back all the billions he had borrowed to industrialize the country. He exported everything, especially food. You had to get up at five o'clock in the morning to get two litres of milk for your kids. Food rations became the norm. Meat, oil, sugar, flour, and other products simply weren't available. We heard that a man once bought a fridge and a friend asked him, "What are you going to put in the fridge?" He yelled in the downtown crowd, "I will put Ceausescu in it." The next day, he was gone and nobody heard of him again.

All agricultural land was taken away from the owners. People had to work in co-ops all summer long, and seventy-five percent of the produce was exported in the fall without the workers being paid for it. The rest was divided among the co-op members.

It was very hard to make a living. A family might have to survive a whole year on nothing more than four kilograms of flour, two kilograms of sugar, and three litres of oil. And there was no place to buy what you needed. That's why a lot of people from the countryside moved to the big cities. To prevent this huge migration, the Communist Party made a rule: you could only live in a city if you were born there or if you married somebody who lived there.

All production planning and budgeting came from the top of the government for each and every company. Bragging about high production performances became normal.

Romanians used humour as a means of coping with the hardships of their lives. For instance, the manager of one co-op discussed his dilemma with his assistant, saying, "The directive came from the Party that our sow should produce twelve piglets, but it only produced two. How can I report only two?"

"Well, you cannot do that," said the assistant. "You have to report twelve."

And so they did. The second directive came down from the Party: the first two piglets were to go to the export, and the rest could go to the people!

There were power shortages also. The President wanted to save electrical power, so the order would come from Bucharest, the capital, to cut all power for the population two hours a day, from 5:00 p.m. to 7:00 p.m. That was the time when people were trying to cook supper after working a long day.

I remember a mother who had to warm up milk for her baby, but there was no power. She poured rubbing alcohol on the inside of a large lid, lit it up, and warmed the milk in a cup on that small flame. The sad part was that there were a lot of power plants in Romania; the country was heavily industrialized, but the population only used two percent of the total output.

The power outages, instead of having the saving effect intended, ended up having a wasting result in the big plants. If the order to cut power came unexpectedly, a whole batch of bread would be wasted in bakery ovens. Doctors didn't have the lights on in the hospital at certain hours, so they had to operate with flashlights.

I worked in a five-thousand-employee factory called the Red Jersey—or, as we called it, the Red T-shirt. We made thousands of t-shirts, underwear, pants, and jogging outfits. Big rolls of fabric were knitted on enormous machines and then placed in huge vats of hot paint. The power would sometimes be cut off before the colouring process was finished, thus a lot of waste occurred. None of that was ever reported.

The heat was cut off from people's apartments. In the wintertime, the joke was that nobody was allowed to open the windows, or else the pedestrians would freeze to death. There were a lot of people walking around at any given time who could've potentially frozen to death!

Romania is 238,000 square kilometres and has twenty-two million people. Compared to Canada, it is a small country—only five hundred kilometres by eight hundred kilometres—but the population of Romania and Canada is almost the same.

Everything in the country was government-controlled. We weren't allowed to have passports. If you had one, the police station would keep it. We weren't allowed to travel abroad. You could have gone to Russia, but nobody wanted to, because it was a communist country as well, and even worse than ours. You couldn't go to the United States, Canada, West Germany, or anywhere else in the free world. People tried. Some succeeded, some went to jail, and others died.

There is a story of a guy who tried to escape and ended up in the madhouse.

"Why are you here?" someone in the madhouse asked him. "We know that if you try to escape, you end up in jail."

"Oh yeah," the man said, "but I tried to escape to Russia!"

Ceausescu's right-hand man was Ioan M. Pacepa. He wrote a book, called *The Red Horizons*, that describes life in Romania under the communist regime. He and his daughter weren't allowed to be out of Romania at the same time. He defected to the United States in 1978, but I believe that life in Romania deteriorated much further after he left.

Freedom of religion was another sore spot in our atheistic country. The Communist Party didn't believe in God and they insisted that the people share the same ideology. A lot of times, though, God was our only resource. If I wanted to buy plain wrapping paper, nothing fancy, I couldn't! There was no wrapping paper anywhere to buy! There were no napkins, paper towels, sandwich bags, or brown bags. You couldn't find toilet paper, toothpicks, or even the bare necessities. Therefore, if I worked in a place that produced or used paper, I had to be a very, *very* strong believer not to simply help myself. Yet our churches were strong and we were encouraged never to steal.

We had to live with that dilemma on a daily basis. We needed chicken or eggs and we worked in chicken complexes where there were thousands of chickens or millions of eggs, yet we weren't supposed to touch them—but there was no place to buy them.

We would go to church and pray for God to help us. People in the Western world wanted to help, but the doors to the country were locked shut. Some people tried to smuggle letters to the outside world, but it was risky. We loved to listen to Radio Free Europe or the Voice of America, but we took a chance by doing so. We didn't want to be caught!

Once, all the believers in our factory were called to a large office. We were given papers and pens and told to write a letter to an imaginary friend. I became suspicious and didn't know what to write. Many months later, I realized that they wanted to have a sample of our handwriting in case we sent letters outside Romania. Every letter and phone call that went in or out of Romania was censored.

The services in our churches were government-regulated as well. After years of churches being locked up, they let us worship on Sunday morning, Sunday evening, and Friday evening. There was a time when we couldn't have a worship service on Sunday evening unless there was a wedding or special occasion, so families would plan a wedding on a Sunday evening just to be able to have a church service.

The government also wanted our pastors to work with the Securitate (the secret police) to turn believers in, especially if someone wanted to escape. If the pastor didn't comply, they took away his preacher's licence, meaning he couldn't preach and feed his family. If he did comply, he felt like Judas. They belittled us, put us down, mocked us, and played with us like a cat with a mouse, forcing us to make tough decisions. They tried to get people to become Party members, but there was no benefit in doing that. You only had to attend long, phony Party meetings.

If you were a believer, it was nearly impossible to get a decent job, even if you had the education for it. I had graduated from a school that combined high school with a business administration program. After four years, I had both a high school and accountant diploma. Everywhere I went as a believer, however, they knew me and kept an eye on me. Teachers in school knew that I was a Christian, so my homeroom teacher would say to me, "Come on, say the lesson, and don't give me a sermon like in your church!"

When I got hired at the Red T-shirt, they knew right away that I was a Christian, and because of that I wasn't given a TA (technical administrative) job. I inquired at the office about getting one, but the boss there told me that I had to give up my faith first. He whispered to me, "You have to shake hands with the devil if you want to cross the bridge," meaning that I had to agree to a shady deal before getting what I wanted.

Once, while on vacation on the Black Sea shore, eight hundred kilometres from home, I saw an advertisement for a day trip to Bulgaria, the neighbouring communist country to the south. I decided I wanted to go. You had to apply ten days ahead of time, so they could check your record. My request was denied. The reason? My younger brother was in university to become an opera singer. He had travelled with the opera choir to perform in a few large cities in Europe, Berlin being one of them. He was only allowed to go because he had left his wife and daughter behind in Romania. After struggling a whole night, he decided to defect to West Berlin anyway. Because my brother remained in the free world at that time, I wasn't allowed to go to Bulgaria. The communists were afraid that I, too, would run away from Bulgaria to Greece.

It may sound as if I'm just running a litany of complaints, but this was the very harsh reality for most of the Romanian people. They were getting desperate. They wanted improvements, but the Party refused. Believe it or not, the Party wanted to recruit new members just to prove how good we had it. And I was about to find out.

In 1975, I was called to go see Jena, a secretary of the Youth Party in the factory where I worked. It smelled fishy, but I had no choice but to go.

THE *Church*

3

Jena had a small, well-equipped office next to the Planning
Office. Afraid and timid, I knocked on the door.

"Enter!" I heard from inside.

I gulped hard and walked in.

Jena had a beautiful face, which I knew well, although I
had tried to avoid her. Her big, dark brown eyes contrasted
her blond, shoulder-length hair. She was of medium build and
height and had a rich, rather low voice. But she could be warm
when she wanted to.

"How is it going?" she asked.

"Good," I replied, still uneasy.

"Why didn't you come to the Party meeting last Wednesday?"

I was shocked. "I'm not a member of the Party, and I don't think I have to be there!"

"And why aren't you a member of the Party?"

"I never wanted to be one."

"The Party sent you to school and gave you an education," she said. "That means you have to be a propagandist!"

I barely knew that word. "Propagandist?"

"Yes. You have to be grateful to the Party and be a part of it by joining and then recruiting other people."

She raked me over hot coals for half an hour for not doing my job as a propagandist. I came out of there crying. Looking back now, most likely somebody else had done that to her and she felt like she should pass it on.

After being in Canada for five years, when the communist regime was finally ousted, I heard that Jena became a believer and that she got baptised in the same church I had once gone to. When I heard that, I was mad!

This is so unfair, I thought. *How convenient! Now she goes to church after she shamed me mercilessly for doing the same thing.*

But then I forgave her, and I think she did well. Are we not supposed to forgive our enemies? In fact, here's what I learned after so many years in church: we have to do good to those who treat us badly. But this is a lot easier said than done.

Church was a big part of my life. I was born in the church. Well, not really; I was born in the hospital, but my parents were members of the Sperantza Church, one of the three or four Baptist churches in Arad. When I was nine, I joined the orchestra with other kids my age. My older brother, Costica, six years my senior, played guitar. My younger brother, Avram, now an opera singer in Germany, played accordion. When he was about nine years old, he played the accordion in his class at school. His teacher, a fine lady, loved him to pieces for doing that.

I played in the church's string orchestra for about seven years. We all went to practices gladly, because we enjoyed playing the instruments. We had fun. The orchestra conductor, Ady, later married one of my best friends, a beautiful girl.

Ady was a tall, lanky young man who liked to conduct the orchestra with large, sweeping motions. One Sunday morning while we were playing, his hands caught his music sheets and they flew off the easel. It was hard to continue playing and not laugh, but it was all fine in the end, because we had our music sheets and we knew the song.

When I turned sixteen, I joined the choir. My two brothers did the same. In addition, they played in the brass band, which only had men. The choir and brass band conductor had excellent leadership qualities. His name was Florea Burca, and even today he's renowned for starting up choirs and brass bands all over North America.

As you might have guessed, he left Romania before the fall of communism in 1989. In fact, I remember Maria, his wife, telling me that in 1985, before I left Romania, she once got up at five o'clock in the morning to get some milk. "By the time I waited half an hour in line, the store ran out of milk," she said. She then walked forty minutes to another store, waited in line, and when her turn came—again, there was no more milk! She went to a third store and the same thing happened. She spent six hours and still had no milk! By then she was frozen, so she went to her mother's house and hugged the warm terracotta, a wood-burning stove. "If you can get out of this country, go," she told her husband. "We will follow you." They have one daughter, Mirela, a very good friend of mine.

It happened to many, many, many people, many, many, many times, going to the store and not being able to but what they needed. I don't know why, but for some reason what

Maria said—and the way she said it—got stuck in my brain.

Ah, but we had sweet times of fellowship in the church. It was a place of comfort where you could pour out your heart to the Lord, even if you prayed in silence. The Lord was there. We knew it. The Lord was real to us.

The church soon outgrew the building and we had to build a new one. We faced incredible harassment about that. I don't think I know the half of it. After many years of red tape and huge stumbling blocks, we proceeded with the construction. There were no contractors to hire, so as members we had to do all the work. And we did it gladly and joyfully. Every day, I went to the church site after work and helped. Sometimes I helped a retired bricklayer build the wall. Other times I was a helping hand for the carpenter. Some days, I opened bags of cement and filled the buckets. The cement bags were in a shack, hundreds of them. I had to do the work inside so I wouldn't spread cement dust all over the neighbourhood. The pastor once came by and didn't recognize me, dusty from so many cement bags. He was impressed with how hard-working I was, though.

Whatever we could help with, we did it with all our hearts. I was so very tired going home some days at nine or ten o'clock in the evening that I felt like a mechanical toy. My arms and legs would swing automatically, but I felt like if somebody pushed me, I would lose my balance and collapse. It was a forty-five-minute walk home.

We hired an engineer part-time to give us the specs. He directed us with the correct information about footings, wall thickness, strength, height, and everything else we needed to know to have a beautiful building. I think our pastor once said that our new church was thirty metres long, fifteen metres wide, and ten metres tall. It had ten windows on each long wall. Each window was five metres tall. When the church was completed in 1978, it was one of the biggest of its kind in Europe. For the communist country we were living in, this was a great miracle of God. We hired some painters to decorate the ceiling with an awesome design. It had five partitions, with gold trims around them and an intricate Turkish design in the middle. Five large candelabras with long, curvy arms hung from each partition centre.

I once heard the pastor ask the church if we should spend so much on this new building, about two million lei. One man said, "Brother pastor, we want to have nice houses, but we want the house of our Lord to be the nicest!" Everybody agreed. We all contributed money. A single family paid the entire electrical bill installation—thirty thousand lei. That was a lot of money, but churches couldn't borrow from the bank. For comparison, my monthly wages were about 1500 to 1800 lei.

One week, four visitors came from Hungary, our neighbouring country to the west. They had heard about our church and wanted to see it. As they walked in, each let out an admiring "Ooooooh! Ooooooh! Ooooooh! Oooooooh!"—and in four different pitches.

There was a large balcony in the back, the choir had chairs in the front, and the preacher's pulpit stood in the middle. Behind the pulpit was the baptismal area with a beautiful picture of a river that seemed like it flowed into the baptismal tank. There were a lot of other art decorations, too.

The physical building was very beautiful, but the spiritual church was even more beautiful still. A bond connected us all. Many former members of the church are now spread all over the world, but we like to keep tabs on each other when we can. I feel connected in a special way to all the people I knew there.

For the opening of the new church, many guests came from around the world. The choir, directed by Florea Burca, sang wonderful songs, culminating with the vibrant Hallelujah chorus. We all felt indescribable joy, making us feel like we were in heaven.

There was a lot of activity in the church. Every Sunday morning we had an hour of prayer from 9:00 to 10:00. The next hour was filled with Sunday school, and the whole church participated. From 11:00 until 12:00, we had a worship service. The choir and band participated in every worship service. For the evening service, people sang alone or in groups while others recited poems; the children were active also. It was a joy to be there.

It was in the church that I learned all the valuable lessons of my life. I learned that there is a God you can pray to in the secrecy of your room. I learned that you can tell God anything, even your doubts, even if you doubt His existence. If you are honest and you truly call on God, He will answer you in an unmistakable way. I learned that you have to be true to God and to your word, even if it costs you. I learned that honesty is the best policy. I experienced some powerful examples of that.

At work, I was promoted to work in the Salaries Office after working in the t-shirt plant. When Rita, the manager of the office, was gone on holidays, the remaining nine employees would have a ball, for Rita was very tough.

Once while she was gone, my colleagues decided that each of us should take a day off and be paid for it.

"I can't do that," I said.

They said, "No, you have to, or else we're afraid you're going to squeal on us."

"No, I won't tell on you. I won't tell a soul!"

But they wouldn't let me. "You have to take a day off like the rest of us, so that we know for sure."

Finally, I reluctantly agreed.

During my day off, I found a silk dress in a store that I really liked. It was soft and flowing and I bought it, even though it was seven hundred lei, which represented half a month's wages. The first time I washed that dress, it went horribly out of shape. It was ruined! I had stolen a day off and ended up losing ten times that much! You might say it was just a coincidence, but I know better. I shouldn't have done that. I couldn't stop my colleagues, but I made the wrong choice.

Here's another story about having strong character. There was in our neighbourhood a man named Petrica Teodor who had come back from the war crippled. His left hand was immobilized and always at his side. His left leg was stiff and he dragged it behind him. He had three little daughters; the middle one was my age. His wife had died when the youngest of the girls was six years old, and the oldest was ten years old. He attended the Pentecostal church in town and wasn't able to work.

I knew from my parents that a number of churches had collected funds to build a house for this very needy family. Apparently my parents contributed five hundred leis, almost a month's wages at that time. When I was twenty-two years old, Mr. Petrica came for a visit. We never really visited each other. Mr. Petrica always spoke like Moses; he stuttered terribly. We were very surprised by his visit and anxious to know the purpose of it.

"H–h–h–h–hi," he said. "H–h–h–how ar–r–re you?"

"Oh, we're fine, thank you," Mom said. "How are you?"

"G–g–g–good."

I didn't feel like asking any questions. It took a long time to get the answer!

"I–I–I–I came t–t–t–to thank you."

"For what?" Dad asked.

Mr. Petrica wanted to thank my parents for the help given fifteen years earlier. His daughters had married, and he had married, too. Now he wanted to pay back my parents those five hundred lei. My mom burst into tears. She was scrounging up all the money she could to cover the down-payment for my brother's apartment. My brother had gotten married and he and his wife wanted to buy an apartment, but they had to pay off one quarter of the apartment before the bank would give them a mortgage for the rest. They needed fifteen thousand lei—fast.

Mr. Petrica brought such a comfort to us. It didn't pay the whole amount, far from it, but we knew there was a God who would see us through all our needs. Mr. Petrica didn't have to pay us back. Nobody had expected that. Since he paid us, I'm convinced that he also tried to pay everybody else who had helped him. He didn't know about our financial strain, but God knew. In my book, Mr. Petrica is a champion!

When I say that he was a stammerer, I'm not mocking him. It is a fact of life. Did you hear about the stuttering Bible School student who had to sell Bibles? He had the biggest sales. His classmates asked him how he managed that, to which he replied, "I–I–I–I ask p–p–p–people i–i–i–if they w–w–w–want t–t–to buy the B–B–B–B–Bible or i–i–if they w–w–want m–m–me to r–r–r–read it to them."

In the church, I saw a new face—a young, well-dressed man with a leather jacket and a yellow scarf around his neck. He was about to call my name.

MY *Husband*

4

Every Sunday evening after church, the youth went for a walk downtown. Running between the nursing school and the theatre was a long walkway so wide that twelve people could link arms and walk side by side. For an hour or two we walked and talked, up and down, and watched who was going with whom.

One Sunday in March, I was walking with three girlfriends when we saw a new face by the theatre. It was the man with the yellow scarf I had seen earlier in church! He came close to us and called out to me: "Come! Come here, darling!"

I was very surprised, but I went to him and we walked together.

"I need to go home," I said after awhile.

"I'll walk with you."

"I live far away, in Gradiste." That was the name of my suburb.

He said, "I know."

"You know? How come?"

"Oh, I just know," he replied.

We walked home, talking and laughing. He was very funny… he made me laugh lots. He was medium height and very broad-shouldered; his blond hair was parted on the left side and he had blue eyes with long, curled eyelashes. He told me that he was master mechanic and that he had been watching me from a distance for about a year. I was amazed. Later on, I learned that men do that. They watch a girl they want to marry for a few months—or even a year—just so they know who she's going out with, how she's behaving, etc. I never knew that.

When we reached our house, he asked if I would go on a date with him—Tuesday at 5:00 p.m. I agreed.

On Tuesday, it was raining really hard when I arrived at the bank, our prearranged meeting place. I was there; he was not. When I got home, he was in our house! He explained to me that he had been helping his landlord, Mr. Vlad, and was too embarrassed to excuse himself and leave a job half done. He tried to get to the bank once the job was finished, but it was too late, so he hurried to my house instead.

When I walked in, I was shocked to see him seated at the table with a plate of food in front of him and my mom questioning him:

"What is your name?"

"How old are you?"

"Where do you work?"

"What are your wages?"

I was embarrassed that my mom was interrogating him, but I noticed that he answered all her questions with ease and enjoyment. It was like they were playing a game!

Then I found out some things about him that I hadn't known. For example, he told my mom that his name was Ioan (pronounced ee-one), the Romanian form of John. He was twenty-five years old and worked for Avicola, a huge chicken complex where they produced eighteen thousand chickens and thousands of eggs.

"Where are you from?" Mom continued after he revealed his wages. "How about your parents? Do you have brothers? Sisters? Do you go to church? Are you baptised?"

He answered all these questions cheerfully. No, he wasn't baptised yet, but he planned to do so at the first baptism at the church.

He kept coming around and we got to know each other a little better.

However, Mom noticed a roughness in him. "He's not for you," she started telling me.

He began to talk about marriage. "I always wanted to get married when I was twenty-five years old," he said. "I'm twenty-five now and I want to marry you."

I felt that I was in a bind. He was saying yes, but Mom was saying no. What was I to do? Mom had noticed that his Christianity wasn't very deep; she saw his flaws and she was worried. I was convinced that even if he wasn't that good of a Christian, I could change him. For sure I could! I would be such a good example that it would be impossible for him not to become a good man of God. My mom and dad weren't very happy.

I felt that he was pressuring me so much that I couldn't say anything but yes. He wouldn't take no for an answer. So we talked wedding.

At Romanian weddings, it's customary to hire a chef and get all the relatives and neighbours to help. I still remember the day I found rice at a store three kilometres away. What a great joy! We needed it for cabbage rolls. I bought twenty kilograms (forty-four pounds). I couldn't leave it there or it would have been gone in half an hour. The weight of that sack of rice stays with me to this day. It was unbearably hard to carry! At the time, I only weighed sixty kilograms. Just imagine carrying a burden one-third of your weight for three kilometres. I shall never forget it as long as I live, but with an indescribable effort I did bring it home.

It was a foretaste of the hardship I would have to go through.

On a cold October day, we got married. I had started work just one week prior to my marriage. My working days started at 6:20 every morning. It was very hard. When I had been in school, I'd started classes at 8:00 a.m. Now school was done and I had to work as an unqualified labourer because of my faith. It was rough, physical work and I had to get up very early in the morning, which I wasn't used to.

I remember that I had to fling heavy packages of sweaters three meters up onto a high shelf—I did that all day long until I was kaput. Add to that a young man freshly married who never had enough of it and all the household duties I now had to do—like cooking, doing laundry by hand, and cleaning... well, it was a lot. I started losing weight, and not on purpose. In six months, I lost fifteen pounds and I looked like a scarecrow. My neighbours didn't recognize me on the street. At the time, it was not in fashion to be that skinny.

We lived with my parents. So did my older brother, who was married and had two little daughters. My younger brother was working and taking evening classes.

I started to notice that my husband would flare up over small things. I also heard him say that I didn't have to be in church all day long—an hour either in the morning or in the afternoon was good enough. When I heard him say that, my heart cringed. Church? That was my social life, my entire life. That was where I drew my strength. Giving that up would be like pulling my heart out of my chest. I couldn't do that. I couldn't betray the God I had trusted up until now.

I had also noticed that lately my husband kept saying things like, "If you don't do as I say, we'll separate!" Every so often I heard that. Where was the man who had so much wanted to marry me? It made me think that the only reason he had married me was to be able to live and work in the city, as he had been born in a village. Why else was he talking separation so soon?

I couldn't believe it, but I observed with horror that a new stage was beginning to take place in my life.

Unravelling

5

On May 2, 1972, a spring holiday in Romania, and six months after our marriage, it was customary for people to go out for picnics. We went to a place called The Three Islands, a picturesque place by the River Mures, a large river that flows by Arad. There were a lot of large trees, bushes, and many flowers. The place was crowded.

After we ate, he grabbed me by the feet (I was in a swimming suit) and held me above the deep and rapidly flowing river for thirty seconds. I didn't know how to swim and it terrified me to look at the water upside-down. A lot of people had drowned in there because of the strong underwater currents. The water was five meters below the abrupt shore.

"Are you crazy?" I said. "What did you do that for? What if you dropped me! I would've drowned or broken my neck! Would you have looked after me for the rest of my life?"

We had a big argument and then went home.

The next morning, we argued about the same thing. He kept asking, "Why did you call me crazy?"

I stuck to my side of the story. "Because you held me up-side-down above the river! If you wouldn't have done that, I wouldn't have said it!"

"Don't ever call me crazy again!"

"Then don't hold me up like that again!"

Then my husband slapped my face. I was so bewildered that I fell onto the couch. When I got up, he slapped me again. In a rage, I took the ring off my finger.

"Take everything you have and leave!" I shouted, my face swollen.

We went to work. When we came back, he asked me, "Are you sure you want me to leave? Because if I go, I'll never come back!"

"*Go!*" I said, still angry.

He took a shot of palinka, a kind of hard liquor, grabbed most of his clothes, and moved in with his former landlord. His sister Maria was renting a room there as well.

I usually went to church on Sunday, but now I had no husband. What a shame! How would I tell everyone that I had kicked him out? This was so embarrassing! In that time, people didn't separate as quickly as they do now—especially if they were Christian! Growing up in the church, I had always felt that people who divorced walked backwards.

Oh, what had I done?

I decided to talk to him and ask him to come back. We could still be okay.

Well, it didn't work. I talked to him many, many times, begging him to come back, but he very stubbornly refused. Every week I pleaded with him to forgive me, to come back and be a family again.

"I would be a rug under your feet," I said to him. "You won't have to do anything, I'll do everything. Just come back, please!"

The only thing he'd say to me was, "Undress."

"No!" I'd say, pleading meekly. "That's not why I came. Let's make peace!"

As soon as he got what he wanted, he would kick me out. That happened many, many, many times.

He had moved to a house on the other side of our suburb where there was a pub. That side of town became such a horrible place for me. Going there in the evening, because he worked late, felt like walking through hell. Drunkards made their way home from the pub, wailing and bemoaning loudly in the dark, stray dogs barking… it was such a hated place.

Our parents tried to reconcile us. He wouldn't listen. The pastor tried. It didn't work. The pastor, a kind and gentle man named Ioan Trutza, invited us to his home and prayed with us. He told John many, many times, "John, go back to your wife!" But John was too set in his ways.

We were called to attend meetings with the church board. These old men, who had a lot of standing in our church, tried to persuade him to keep his family. It was useless. One of them told us about a colonel in the army who commanded hundreds of soldiers, yet when he was home he listened to his wife, took the garbage out, and helped her in the kitchen. The rank didn't matter in the family.

We went to see a counsellor at the courthouse, who asked us, "Why do you want to separate?"

"Because she called me crazy."

"Do you think she's unfaithful to you?" the counsellor asked.

"No," replied my man.

"Did you have arguments about money?"

"No."

"Listen, young man, I have been married for eighteen years. You have no reason for divorce! You don't leave your wife because she calls you crazy!"

Mine did. He made me feel so low, so despicable. I was devastated. I lost the joy of living. I became withdrawn and quiet. I felt crushed inside. Small talk was too much for me. For many, many years, I wasn't able to comfortably carry on simple conversations. Just surviving was more than I could bear.

There were days when I wished to die. I couldn't die, though, and I knew that suicide would take me to hell. I had to go on living, so I prayed desperately. I wanted so much to correct what I had done wrong.

Because I had been born on a Tuesday, I started to fast every Tuesday, for a year or two. Many times I would fast a whole week, or ten days in a row. When I fasted, I only ate and drank in the evening. My mom prayed and fasted with me. I knew that prayer and fasting could solve every problem, so I fully expected my husband to come back. Yet it seemed like the more I fasted, the further away he went.

I couldn't understand.

I felt forsaken.

Looking back, I see that our separation wasn't caused by any significant thing. We didn't cheat on each other and we had no major problems. My husband was hard-working, he wasn't a drunkard, he didn't spend money on booze, he didn't chase women, and he didn't steal. He was just too proud and stubborn.

The Bible puts stubbornness on the same level with rebellion and idolatry, according to 1 Samuel 15:23 and Deuteronomy 21:20. It was his stubbornness that led to his downfall.

And being too proud and cocky to accept me back, he fell for something far worse.

Truce

OR TRICK

6

When my husband moved in with his sister, another girl from their village was living in the same house with them. Her name was Nona. Right away, she was after him. In fact, she once told me straight to my face, "I like your husband, I love your husband, I *want* your husband!" And she did whatever she could to have him, like waiting for him in his bed. What could I do? If he accepted her passes, there were the two of them together against me and I couldn't win. The only thing I could do was keep praying and fasting. God was my only hope.

One Friday night, two years after our separation, my husband came to church and told me that he had finally agreed to our reconciliation. Oh, what a great joy! He told me that I had to move in with him to a house out of town. His sister and Nona were going to move with us for a short time, and then they would move somewhere else.

I was elated! Thank God! Finally!

From the edge of town, there were four bus stations leading to that house in the middle of nowhere. The first bus station was by the hot house where John, Maria, and Nona worked. The second bus station was by a cemetery, then the third, and then the house. If you think this was a fancy house, forget it! It was a long building that had been a barn years ago. It didn't even have any electrical power. There were five apartments in it and ours was the last one. The apartment consisted of a very narrow hallway and a large room with one window, a kitchen table, some chairs, and two beds, one on each side of the table. There was one clothes closet, some shelves, and a wood-burning stove. On the east end of the hallway was a gas stove, and on the west end a tiny cold room.

John and I slept in one bed and Maria and Nona in the other. My hopes for our reconciliation were dashed one by one. That was not a family life. He was closer to them than to me. I was invisible to him. Sitting on the bed between the girls, he would tickle and play with them. I would go outside and cry bitterly.

"When are the girls moving out?" I asked him one day.

Soon they did, but so did he. He wouldn't come home, or if he did, he would eat, change his clothes, and leave again. Where? He never told me. Sometimes he would come home after midnight. Most days he didn't come home at all. That happened day after day for two months. I would be waiting for him, crying in my pillow so the neighbours wouldn't hear. Either that or I would softly play my mandolin.

I couldn't eat. I didn't feel like doing anything. My life was stalled. While I was living there, he went to the courthouse and filed for divorce without telling me.

One of the neighbours asked me one day, "Why are you living here? I heard that your parents have a big house in town."

"Yes, they do," I said, "but I want to be with my husband."

The neighbour just grunted when he heard that.

Easter was coming. On the Saturday before Easter, John told me that if I wanted to have a quiet holiday, I should move back with my parents.

That day, I moved back. My guess was that someone had advised John to pretend like he wanted me back, but then conduct himself in such a way that I would leave on my own; that way, he would have a reason to file for divorce.

It broke my heart to go to the courthouse for divorce, but John didn't even show up! The judge asked me where he was. I didn't know. Every time we had to go to the courthouse, he was a no-show. Finally, his request for divorce was rejected as unsupported.

Very shortly after I moved home, John and Nona moved in together.

Praying
FOR MY EX

7

It's so hard to feel rejected! You feel like you're worth nothing and would do anything to prove your worth. I couldn't understand why God didn't respond to me and solve my case. I knew that God was there, and I knew that He heard my prayers. Why such a long delay? I decided to keep praying for my ex until he came back!

Somebody once said to me, "God did answer your prayer, but you didn't understand!"

"Okay," I said. "I'll give you that. Maybe God did answer me and I didn't understand. But He's God! If that's the case, He knows that I didn't understand. Why then doesn't He answer me in a way that I do understand?"

She couldn't answer me.

I kept praying, fasting, and hoping. Yet nothing happened. I was alone, alone, alone. Whether I went to church, to a wedding, or to a funeral, I felt like the fifth wheel on a car. When I was with my family, there was always Mom and Dad, Costica and Florica, Avram and Aurica, and I was alone. I didn't date anyone; I didn't have any intimate relationships. Around me kids were growing up, getting married, having families, and I was still single.

In the summer of 1974, I went on vacation to the Black Sea coast for a student camp. I found some friends there—two boys and a girl. Hank, Steven, Nelly, and I went shopping, played volleyball on the beach, and had fun together. I tried to forget all my sorrows. I wasn't looking for any new relationship, though. I was hurting too much from my old one.

One day, we found out that it was Nelly's birthday. We went to a big gift shop to buy something for her as a surprise. She liked a tin face of a man with a pipe and wanted to buy it.

"I'm sorry, this is mine!" Steven said. It was the only one.

Nelly was mad that Steve wouldn't let her have "the piper," as we called it.

I bought a card, and then we went for lunch. I told them to go ahead, because I wanted to take a shower.

Nelly got mad at me, too. "What's the matter with her? Why does she want to take a shower now?"

They left and I arranged the gift and card on the table. When they came back, she was stunned! Our little surprise made her day and we had fun talking about it.

Once, when we had about ten people over to our room, everyone was passing around a postcard. I wanted to see it, too. It was for me! My brother Avram had sent it and asked me to buy some flip-flops. He had addressed it Lidia Sturz, my maiden name, instead of Pater, my husband's name. I wasn't divorced, so everybody knew me as Lidia Pater. Everybody got quiet in the room. I didn't say anything. So much for leaving my troubles at home! They seemed to have followed me. A few months later, I met Nelly in my hometown and she asked about my last name. I told her the truth and she confided that all my friends had thought I was adopted.

In 1978, I went to Timisoara, the closest town to ours, except it was bigger. I went to the jail to visit a girl named Flora. Her parents were cousins of my parents. She had been the manager of a store, and after a while it was found out that she had stolen something like a hundred thousand lei. She had been sentenced to nine years!

Flora wasn't a Christian and I barely knew her, but I went with her mother. I brought her three gladioli flowers for no reason, but then found out that she would turn thirty in three days. The guards didn't allow her to keep the flowers, not even in the waiting room, so I had to take them back. When I was taken inside to see her, there were two glass walls between us and a guard patrolled back and forth. We couldn't even touch each other.

In December 1982, I was sent to Bucharest to perform an audit in a factory. I had to go on behalf of someone from the Control Financial Intern office. All the ladies in our office were married and had children, so, being single, I was designated to go.

Even though Romania was communist, most people wanted to have a Christmas tree for Christmas. We always decorated the tree with special Christmas candies made with soft fudge wrapped in coloured foil with white fringes on the ends. But being in Romania, you just couldn't buy those. Over the phone, I told my colleagues that the candies were available in Bucharest. They all wanted some, so I had to buy sixteen kilograms (thirty-five pounds) of the stuff.

Now remember, it was December, wintertime, so I had a heavy coat, boots, and lots of luggage. I was in Bucharest for two weeks and the candy store was two steps away from my hotel, but I was getting worried; how could I take the candies home? The city was overcrowded, so I had to take the bus and the train to get around. You couldn't get on a bus even without any luggage, but I would somehow have to do it. I bought the candies and the store clerk put them in a huge box. I carried it to the hotel, then tried to get to the elevator, because my room was on the second floor. That's when I saw in the hallway my neighbour from back home, Stefan Purdi. He was a driver for emergency vehicles. He told me that he had come to Bucharest to get some medication for the hospital in Arad, our hometown.

"What are you doing with those candies?" he asked.

"I bought them for my colleagues back home."

"I can take them home for you."

"Oh, thank you!"

He took the box to his car and took them home. No more hassle for me. What a relief! If I would've been thirty seconds later in that hallway, I would have missed him. Now *that* was God's timing!

On my way back from Bucharest, I stopped by Jebel, a large town two hours away from home, to visit relatives. It was midnight when I got to my uncle's house, but they couldn't hear me knock, so I walked forty minutes to get to my aunt's place. The night was very dark but warm and the stars were huge, very bright and very close. I felt that if I reached up on my toes, I could pluck them out of the sky. It was like a metaphor for my life; I felt unresolved, walking in the dark, but the presence and wonders of God were very close to me. I shall never forget the stars that night, how many, how bright, and how close they were.

I really wanted to be married and to have a family. I couldn't understand why this wasn't happening yet, but I trusted God deeply. I kept praying for my ex; we were still married. After six or seven years of waiting, though, I became sceptical that he would ever come back. I heard that he and Nona were still living together, but their life was hell on earth. They had a son together. Many people asked me why he had left me for her. Usually a person moves on to a better-looking or more educated person than the one they had before, but not in John's case. He was very ashamed to go home to see his parents, because Nona's family didn't have a good name in their village. My in-laws regretted terribly the fact that he had left me. My father-in-law even came to our church once and cried on my shoulder.

One year in the fall, when women make pickles and preserves for the winter, my mother-in-law sent my father-in-law to visit John and Nona with two large bags. His mission was to bring back empty jars, as she had sent pickles and preserves to them sometime earlier. You couldn't buy the jars in the store, so people saved them. When my father-in-law arrived, he found out that Nona had given the leftover jars to her own mother and only had two jars left.

My father-in-law became enraged. Just the sight of her made him incensed. He took the two jars, went out into the yard, and with all the bitterness accumulated in his heart took one jar, lifting it into the air.

"Lord Almighty," he said, "if you would make it in your mercy that my son would separate himself from this woman, then may this jar not break!"

He smacked the jar with all his might against the trunk of an old tree. The jar chipped at the mouth, but only very slightly. Very encouraged, he lifted the second jar.

"And Lord, if you would bring back my son and *his wife* to be a family, then make this jar break into a million pieces!"

He brought the jar down against the tree and it broke into a million pieces. From that point on, my father-in-law lived with the hope that we would be together, though he never lived to see it. In 1983, a cart full of logs fell on him and he died.

All of John's family was very fond of me and sad when we broke up.

A young woman from the church named Hortensia once told me an interesting story. In 1984, she was shopping in Timisoara when a young man approached her and said, "Excuse me, but are you from Arad?"

"Yes, I am," she said. She was surprised at his attention since she was eight months pregnant at the time. If a man was after a woman, he wasn't going to go for such a pregnant one.

"Are you from Church Sperantza?" When she said that she was, he continued, "My sister-in-law Lidia, what do you know about her? Is she okay?"

"Oh, she's fine," Hortensia said.

The man, John's younger brother Mitru, smiled. "I just wanted to say hello to Lidia."

Mitru drowned a month after that at the age of twenty-nine. I never saw him again.

John also had a little sister named Nicoleta who was twenty years younger than him. She was very friendly, a sweet five-year-old little girl. She stuck to me like glue.

"Mommy," she once asked her mother, "why did you put Johnny and Lidia to sleep in separate beds the first time they came to our house, and you put them in the same bed the second time?"

I had visited them before and after our wedding.

Maria, John's sister who lived with us for a while, told me that she had been so oblivious that she had no idea something was going on between Nona and her brother until they moved in together. Maria then went after Nona and shamed her mercilessly: "Aren't you ashamed of yourself? Shame on you for breaking up my brother's family. Why did you do that?" Maria couldn't stand her anymore.

The three of them—John, Nona, and Maria—worked together in a hot house. John and Nona were working together in the mushroom section, and the other workers apparently saw them very close together. For that reason, I couldn't eat mushrooms for many years, even though I liked them. Fortunately, I'm over that now.

After he moved in with Nona, John stopped going to church. He lived a worldly life.

"I want to build a brick house," he said to me once. "I want you to sign a paper that you give up any right you might have on it, or else I'll curse you with every brick I lay."

I was disgusted by his cruelty.

"Who wants your house?" I asked.

He never built it.

I kept going to church and trusting God, even though it seemed like an impossible task to have my family back. Because we were separated, though not divorced, we were excommunicated from the church. I couldn't sing in the choir or take communion.

A lady from my office told me that she had friends living next door to John and Nona's apartment. Apparently there was so much turmoil in John's apartment that the neighbours had to move away. Plates with food would fly out the window. I heard that she was very mean to him. Apparently when he wanted to go to his cousin's wedding, she soaked all his clothes in the bathtub so he couldn't go.

Well, it serves him right, I thought. *She can skin him alive for all I care.*

In 1978, when their son was three years old, I went to the courthouse and officially divorced him. I gave up hope of him ever coming back. He was already telling his mother things like, "I'm divorced from Lidia, but I will never marry Nona. Never!"

Much later, John told me that he'd known going with her was the wrong thing to do. Yet he had felt tied up. She had given him something to drink that kept him from thinking straight; apparently she and her mother were very involved in witchcraft. He felt that he stayed with her against his will, that there was nothing he could do. Well, if you're a strong believer, the power of the devil may try to attack you, but you'll be protected if you're a child of God. If you're not, the devil will tie you up and render you powerless.

Seven years of waiting was enough.

I won't wait for him anymore, I thought. *I better start praying for my next husband.*

Praying
FOR MY NEXT

8

A s hard as it is to be rejected by your most beloved, you cannot stay that way for the rest of your life. You have to move on. I tried to do that. Although I couldn't understand why God didn't restore my family, I still went to Him with my request for a new husband. As much as I hated to be divorced, I had to accept it. I had to walk backwards.

I made a mental list: *Lord, I'd like my next husband to be a Christian, first of all. A true Christian. I want him to love and appreciate me, to respect me, and to be kind to me. I'd like a tall and handsome guy who can sing well so we can harmonize.*

I didn't ask that he be rich or have a big house and fancy car. We could get those together.

There were lots of guys around. By the time I made my list, I totally excluded John from it. He'd had his chance and blown it.

When I had been in high school, I kind of dated a guy named Jessie. He was tall, with dark curly hair and blue eyes. My mom hadn't wanted me to date anyone until I finished school, though, so we mostly wrote letters to each other. Eventually, we stopped.

After my failed marriage, I was very, very careful. There's a saying in Romanian: if you get burned by soup, you're going to blow everything from then on, even yogurt. People tried to approach me. They didn't know that I was still praying for my husband. In the course of time, however, there came many men knocking on my door. None of them seem to be the right man. I prayed and fasted a day for each and every one who asked me to marry him. The answer was always no, no, no. I didn't date any of those guys. There was no point in dating.

After I divorced John, I was accepted back as a member in our church, because he was living with another woman. I sang in the choir and I recited poems. Our church had about a thousand members back in the early 80s. Going to and from church, I saw couples together holding hands, or the man putting his hand on his wife's shoulder. It was hard. I longed for a relationship. To hold hands! It would've been bliss. A kiss? That would have been like a honeymoon. I was always alone, alone, alone.

Even though there were thousands of people around me, I was like an island. I could have had a man if I wanted, but I desired to keep myself pure for that elusive husband. I'm sure people judged me. Just like Job, I couldn't tell them I was innocent. Even our pastor asked me once, "Lidia, can you still take it being single?" He was a kind and gentle man.

One time, I saw my mom talking to a lady who I recognized as being the mother of one of my classmates from grade school.

"How is Itzu?" I asked the woman. Itzu was Hungarian for the name Ileana.

"She's okay," she told me. "How about you? Are you married?"

"No, my husband left me eight years ago and I'm not with anyone."

She was surprised. "You didn't go with anybody since he left?"

"No!" I replied.

"Oh, Itzu went with three hundred, at least! She has four children and she has no idea who the father is for any of them. Every chance she gets, she runs to the bar. I try to keep her home."

In Romania, if a woman had four children, she was allowed to have abortions. There were no birth control pills. I remembered a beautiful gypsy woman coming to our office once. She was one of the janitors in the factory. Elisabeth was her name. She told us with a beautiful smile that she'd had six children and thirty-three abortions. She was only thirty-three years old. She was married and her husband worked in our factory as well.

A cousin of mine, kind of an ungodly man, came once for a visit. When he heard how my husband treated me, he said, "Give me his address. I will beat him up so bad that he'll be a vegetable for the rest of his life! And he'll never know who did it."

"No, leave him alone," I said. "I don't want anything to do with him."

There was another young man, George, who really wanted to meet me. He had two cousins living further down my street, so he came to our house a couple of times. When we were alone once, he grabbed me, pulling me hard, and tried to kiss me. Yuck! His lips were red, swollen, and hot. I pushed him away as hard as I could. He tried again and again and again.

"Don't ever try!" I told him. "I kiss no man unless he is my husband or husband-to-be."

I thought he would dislike the fact that I had rejected him, but he said, with a dreamy look, "Will you keep being that way?"

I guess he thought that he could trust me. There was something in him that reminded me of my ex and I didn't like that.

I fasted for him to see if he was the one. I hoped not. He told me that he had dreamed we were walking down the road but didn't get to the end of it. I said, "Well then, that's it. There's no point in us trying, because we won't be together."

For another guy, I dreamed that we were shooting at a target but missed.

There was in our church yet another good-looking man, but he was quite a bit older than me. His name was Joe Lurky. He was tall with dark hair, brown eyes, and a solid build. When he first spoke to me, he seemed pleasant. He told me that he used to teach boys at a trade school, but now he fixed coffee machines for all the cafeterias in town. He started to walk home with me and bring me chocolates, cans of pineapple, oranges, and all sorts of other things you couldn't normally buy.

Joe was divorced and had been single for many years. I felt that he was very shrewd. He never forced me into anything, but with all the gifts I felt he was trying to buy my integrity. For instance, I told him that my coffee grinding machine was broken and asked if he could fix it.

"Bring it over," he said.

"Wouldn't you like that? Me, a single woman, going to your apartment, a single man!"

"Just come in the yard and yell at me to come out!" There were at least forty families living there. "Why don't you want to come to my apartment? Are you afraid of yourself?"

As if I couldn't control myself!

So I went. He told me that he was nervous. He would go to get some tool from the kitchen, then forget what he wanted to get.

"Don't you try anything with me or I'll crack your skull," I told him.

I was mean, but I didn't know how to keep myself from falling into sin with him. It wasn't his style to force me, but I didn't know him well. I prayed and fasted for him as well. I had a few dreams that weren't good. In one dream, I was walking with him and wore some white, knee-high socks that got all muddy. In another dream, I splashed my legs with mud while we were walking together. He didn't like hearing about my dreams. They made him mad.

Being with him was like the forbidden fruit. He was very pleasant and had good manners, but he was leading me in the wrong direction.

One other dream I had: I was trying to write a postcard to him. As I wrote "I wanted to tell you that…" the letters suddenly fell down at the bottom of the row and, like worms, they wiggled out of the postcard. I tried again and saw how two of the letters—an "i" and a "v"—became horizontal straight lines and crawled away. Then an "o" split at the top and turned into a wiggly line which ran out with all the other letters.

I tried to tell him that we should stop seeing each other, but he didn't want to hear that. "Why can't a man and woman be friends, just friends?" he kept asking.

He's right! I thought. *Why can't we be just friends?*

I tried. Believe me, I tried hard to be just friends. From my experience, however, that kind of friendship always leads to physical intimacy—and that's called sin. I *did not* do it, but it was very hard. Although it didn't show, he was twenty years older than me. He didn't push for marriage, because he was afraid I would leave him later on.

At the time, there was another man who was madly in love with me, although I didn't care for him. His name was Eli Lascau. He was slim with blond hair and bright blue eyes. I forget how I met him, but he didn't come to church. If he came, it wasn't out of conviction but out of interest. He was a bus driver. He came to my house once or twice, and I could see that he was extremely nervous. He made big gulps when he talked. It amused me to see him like that, but I had no feelings for him whatsoever.

At times, I would take the bus to go to church and Eli was usually the driver on our route. One Friday evening around 6:30, he stopped at the bus station closest to my house. He was waiting for me to go to choir practice. He waited for two hours and told people that the bus was broken! The choir practice had actually been on Thursday, but he was lost in his love. Another time, he stopped the bus with the front door right in front of me, so I had to go in and stand by him, even though we were supposed to get on the bus by the back door and off the bus by the front door. Standing by him while he drove wasn't a good thing. He forgot to stop at the bus stations and people started yelling and accusing me. He told me that a lot of times he was predisposed to accidents because of me. I didn't like that.

Joe, meanwhile, had bought a car. That was very rare in Romania, since it was expensive to buy a car and difficult to get a driver's licence. He had tried twice already. As he was a teaser,

I teased him right back: "Oh my goodness, you were a teacher at a college and you aren't even able to get your driver's licence! I have a friend who's a bus driver! Imagine that! Blond hair and blue eyes! You should see him!"

"Blond hair and blue eyes!" Joe said back. "I'll get after my father. Why didn't he give me yellow hair and blue eyes? It wouldn't have cost him anything!"

By no means was Eli better looking that Joe, but he didn't know that.

Eli once got a good beating because of my teasing. It was a Saturday night and Joe was at our house. It seemed as though he had just forgotten to go home. It was past 11:30 and he still didn't move. By midnight, he left. That same night, Eli got a beating as he was leaving the bus depot. He said that two or three thugs attacked him for no reason, hitting him hard, especially in the face. His nose was so swollen that he didn't come around me for two weeks. I had a great suspicion that the whole affair had been arranged by Joe, but I didn't know for sure and couldn't prove it.

My best friend and colleague from the office, Mary Ro, gave me some very good advice regarding Joe. But as Mary would say, you have to hear the story from the beginning.

Mary Ro

9

There were ten ladies working in the Salaries Office. We handled the payroll for all five thousand factory employees. The office had three windows and the door was opposite the middle window. As you walked in the door, my desk was first, and next to it, by the middle window, was Mary's desk. In front of us were four desks grouped together. Behind us were four more desks grouped together. Rita, the office manager, was seated at one of the desks in front of us. The phone was right where the manager was.

The seating arrangement gave Mary and me some privacy. We started to share more and more of our lives. Mary was six years older than me, born in 1946. She was the youngest of her siblings. Her brother was twenty years older, one sister fifteen years older, and the other ten years older than her. She had come as a surprise in her family, born prematurely at seven months with no fingernails. Her mother had thought she wouldn't make it, but the next day she was still breathing.

Mary was quite chubby, but very witty. She was also an excellent cook; the birthday cakes she made were in high demand. Eyeing Mary's large dress, a lady from the office asked her one day, "Mary, what do you cook in at home?"

"In a caldron!" came a quick retort.

I was walking with my older brother to church one evening when I saw Mary way ahead of us. I told him, "That's my friend Mary. She's a little chubby but very intelligent."

At the office the next day, I told her what I had said to my brother. She wasn't in the least offended. "You should have told him that I'm just as intelligent as I am chubby!"

When she was nineteen years old, a young man came to see her. Mary had a beautiful face, very white skin, and dark brown eyes which often glimmered with playfulness. Back then, she was very thin. Her whole family came home to see this young man and give their opinion about him. When the family left later that day, they waved from the train windows. Their fingers went up and down, meaning, "Yes, we like him!" If they hadn't liked him, they would've waved their hands left to right.

After getting to know her, I started sharing my faith. I told her about God and that we all need a Saviour. No matter who we are, how much or how little we have, we are never really at peace until we're at peace with God. As soon as we surrender to God, everything goes in the right direction—even if there are things we don't understand, like in my case.

I told her about John and how hard I had tried to keep that family. I told her about all the guys who came by my door. Some were too old and not that good-looking, some were too young, some were too short, and at least one was nasty. The nasty one once said to me, "You're good-looking, but I know another one who is class A1! But she has two kids, and I have two kids."

I thought, *Look at him! He talks marriage to me and all the while he's drooling after somebody else… and he has two kids!*

"You know what?" I said. "There never was any business between us and there never will be. Goodbye!"

Mary wanted to know about all those guys. She wanted to see them and give me her honest opinion of them. I tried to do that. She was a valuable friend who understood me and had my best interests at heart.

I told her about Cornel, a good-looking young man from Timisoara who liked to dress in silk shirts. According to my list, he had the looks and the singing voice, but something was missing. As usual, I prayed and fasted for him. I had a dream about him that he was so poor, he didn't even have a shirt on his back. And he was blind, too! I thought for sure he was blind towards me and I never thought about him again after that.

During my vacations from grade school, I used to visit my mom's sister in a town called Jebel. I had been active in the church there. One of the kids named Doru Ilie became very fond of me. He was tall, fine-looking, good with music, and he led the songs in the church. After I was separated from John, he wanted to marry me, but I just couldn't. For one thing he was younger (about one and a half years), but mostly I felt that it wasn't fair for him to get a divorced woman. He kept saying, "I always had you on my left side"—meaning in his heart—but I didn't want to have problems later on because I had been married.

Mary got to see almost all of them, and we would discuss the pros and cons of each one. She started to come to church and became a believer, even getting baptised as a result of our friendship. Her older daughter became a believer, too, and today she lives with her family in Atlanta, Georgia. Mary's sisters turned to God as well, as did her husband.

Coming to church, she got to see Joe Lurky. Mary became very involved with all of my affairs. She even had a dream in which she saw herself in the little Orthodox Church she had grown up in. One Sunday, the priest was making the calls, which means that he was announcing who would be getting married the following week. This time, the priest said, "Next Sunday, Joe and Lidia are getting married. Is that okay?" All the people in the church shouted loudly, "Noooooo!" This wasn't supposed to happen. Usually the priest didn't ask the church; he just announced it. He tried a second time. "Next Sunday, Joe and Lidia are getting married. Is that okay?" Again, all the people shouted, even louder, "Noooooooooooo!" This was becoming embarrassing. Mary then saw that I stood up and told the church that I had been single for ten years, that I had found this man, and that I wanted to marry him. "Is that okay?" I asked. This time, everybody said, "Yes!"

When Mary told me the dream, I was quite baffled. How does one interpret such a dream? What was it supposed to mean? I thought about it for a long time. My conclusion was that the church was the voice of God. God was telling me not once, but twice, not to marry him. But if I really insisted on it, then I could do it. How could I marry someone if God told me two times not to? Was one failed marriage not enough? Oh, how long would I have to wait?

Good
COUNSELLOR

10

Mary and I worked in the same office for twelve years, until I left Romania in 1986. In the course of our job, we had to go to different buildings in our factory to get attendance records to calculate each worker's salary. One morning, I saw Mary in one of the hallways.

"Where are you going?" I asked her.

"Building number one," she told me. "How about you?"

I had to go to the same place, but instead I said, "Where you go, I go. Where you live, I live. Your people will be my people and your God my God. May God do to me whatever, if anything, but death would separate you and me." Then I paused, adding, "I'll tell you a nice story about that when we get back to the office."

Half an hour later, I explained myself.

"In the old days there was a family with two boys that moved from Israel to Moab, the neighbours, because there was a big famine in Israel," I began. "In time the boys got married, but then died—both of them, and their father, too. Now, the mother wanted to go back to Israel and told her daughters-in-law. One said that was okay, but the other said, "No way. I'll go with you." The two of them returned to Israel and the mother-in-law helped her daughter-in-law get married; she even looked after the baby. That baby was David's grandpa!"

Two hours later, Mary had migraines. Her face was pale, her skin was covered in goose bumps, and I could see that she was suffering. She went home and lay down. When Mihaela, her daughter, came home from work, she realised that her mom was suffering from a migraine.

"Mom, can I help you?"

"Read!" Mary said.

Mihaela took the Bible from the night table, opened it to a random spot, and started reading. As she read, she noticed that her mother was crying.

"Mom, are you okay?"

"Yeah."

"Why are you crying?"

She was reading exactly the same story I had told her earlier in the day, but now she heard the whole story with all the names included. It was the book of Ruth from the Bible.

Mary and her husband Mihai had a younger daughter named Dani—short for Daniela, a very charming girl. Every time I went to their house, Dani begged me to sleep over. She would kneel before me or hide my shoes, even though she was about twenty years younger than me. She had a very magnetic personality. The whole family treated me like royalty when I visited.

Mary was a true friend. She didn't hesitate to tell me when I was wrong, and she kept at it until I saw the light. I really appreciated and admired her for that.

One day, I told her that I wanted to go to Bears' Cave, a renowned tourist spot in Romania. Many people from Europe visited that cave. It was three or four hours away and Joe had offered to give me a ride. He had his driver's license by now.

"It's not right for you to go with him!" Mary told me.

"Why not?"

"Because!"

"Oh, leave me alone," I said. "It doesn't mean that I'll go to bed with him! We'll just go there and back!"

"It's not a good idea."

I was irritated. "Just buzz off. You have a husband, you have two daughters, and I'm alone, alone, alone. If I just want to go for the ride, what's wrong with that?"

"You know, the married life isn't always peaches and cream. Your reputation will suffer if you go with him."

I couldn't see why.

"Listen," she said to me. "What would you say if Viorica Florea went with him to Bears' Cave?"

Viorica was a strong believer in our church.

"I would think she's a sleazy woman," I admitted.

I didn't go with Joe to Bears' Cave. Finally, I saw the light.

God used Mary to guide me on the straight and narrow, and she often said the same thing about me. I thank God for her.

It was becoming more and more difficult for me to stay pure. I prayed to God with all my might. If I was about to fall, I needed Him to help me intervene somehow.

"Lord, I don't want to live with anybody. I pray to you now, when I am awake and in the right mind, to say that if you see

57

that I'm losing my head when I'm with Joe, or anybody, don't let that happen! I may be tempted to give in, but please help me!"

God listened to my prayer.

At some point, I really felt ready to give in.

I had gone to town in a give-up mood, thinking, *That's it. If I see Joe, I'll go for it.*

I was in a crowd by the movie theatre when I saw him. I called out to him, but alas, my voice was so soft that he couldn't hear me, and he left! Right away the temptation left, too. I'm so glad that God helped me!

Since separating from John, I didn't sleep with anyone.

"How long do I have to wait?" I prayed to God. "Is there going to be somebody in my life at all? Lord, give me whoever You want. Forget about the list. I'll marry whoever You want me to, even if I don't like him."

For all my longing to be married, I had a quiet and peaceful life with my parents.

We couldn't afford white bread—only "black bread," as we called it. We had no car, so I had to go for a brisk twenty-minute walk every morning to get to work and another twenty to come home. We had meat only once or twice a week. I thought I was deprived, but now, looking back, I know I had the best life.

It was 1984 when I went to the wedding of a cousin of mine also named Lidia. While there, I met a "youngster" who really wanted to talk; he was about twenty-five years old. I was looking for a way to end it, because he was too young, when a woman really did me a favour by asking this guy in private about me: "Do you like her?" she asked. "How old do you think she is?"

He replied, "Twenty-two? Twenty-five?"

"Thirty-two!" the woman said.

His face went deep red to the tips of his ears and he withdrew right away.

At work, people would come by my desk and say, "You didn't get married? Good for you! It's better that way. You go where you want, do what you want."

I knew that whoever said that to me wasn't happy in his or her marriage. There were others, however, who asked, "Why don't you get married? It's so much fun; you don't know what you're missing!"

I wanted to, but would I ever?

One December, I decided to go to one of my cousin's place before my brothers and their wives came home for Christmas. My brothers were always expressing love for their wives, which is a good thing, but this made me feel unattractive and undesirable because I was single. My cousin, Florica Brazovan, was a very fine woman. We had known each other since we were little kids. We had spent a lot of summers together; she was like my sister, seeing that she had a few brothers of her own.

She and her husband loved each other very much, but I never felt excluded or uncomfortable in their home. In fact, they had invited the pastor to come for lunch. Florica asked me to make the dumplings for the soup, but I said, "What if they don't turn out well? I'll be embarrassed." Florica had the same worry.

Her mother-in-law, a very sweet lady, said, "Give them to me. I will make the dumplings." She did and they turned out good.

The pastor was single and looking for a wife. In order to be ordained in Romania, pastors had to be married. He said to Florica, "Too bad your cousin is divorced. I would have liked her." In Romania, a pastor couldn't marry a divorced woman. That's what the Bible said about the priests in Leviticus 21:14.

A lawyer from our factory was a forty-five-year-old single man. Every time he came to our office, my colleagues picked on him. "Mr. Pasha, why don't you get married?"

Once, just to make them shut up, he said, "Well, I proposed to Lidia, but she refused me."

"Mr. Pasha, don't talk wonders!" I told him. That was the same as saying, "Don't talk stupid."

He said, "Listen, Lidia, you're young, you're going to marry, and you're going to have a baby. Then I'm going to ask you, did you make that wonder?"

So it happened that one year later Mr Pasha got married, and another year after that he and his wife had a baby. *I'm going to throw that back at him,* I thought.

I went to his office and asked, "So, Mr. Pasha, did you make that wonder?"

He was embarrassed and apologized. I was still single.

"You don't have to apologize," I said. "I'm not offended. It seemed very unlikely two years ago that you would get married before me and have a baby, but I'm happy for you."

People knew that Christians weren't supposed to cheat, lie, steal, and drink hard liquor, and they often brought it to our attention: "Hey, you're a Christian! *You* aren't supposed to do that!" Well, I tried to live my life right, but I had a dilemma. The girls in our office served sweet liquor for their birthdays. Although I didn't drink it, they did. For each birthday girl in our office, we would each give them thirty lei and buy a significant present. She would then bring some sweets and that liquor. What was I supposed to do? I didn't drink it, but should I buy it for them on my birthday? The answer came with a lot of racket in our factory.

I WILL *Never* SERVE LIQUOR!

11

Payday was the thirteenth day of each month and everything was done on a cash basis. Each employee received his or her pay in an envelope with the name and detailed payroll information written on it. We had to account for certain envelope deductions, which we passed on the designated places. There was an in-house organization called CAR (Casa de Ajutor Reciproc), the House of Mutual Help, which was run by an older, very capable Jewish man named Gyurii Baci (Uncle Gyurii).

CAR provided a simple and efficient loan system for factory employees. Say I needed three thousand lei to buy furniture. I agreed with Gyurii Baci to contribute one hundred lei per month. In ten months, I would have accumulated one thousand lei and then I could borrow three times that total. I would then pay back the three thousand lei in monthly payments—let's say, two hundred lei per month. In fifteen months, I would have paid it all back. Those two hundred lei would be deducted on the envelope, not on the payroll statement. All of those CAR deductions went to Gyurii Baci, who kept a record for each employee who was a CAR member.

One such envelope, containing 2880 lei, was missing from my desk on my birthday, December 16, when I had to give it to Gyurii Baci. Woe to me! The girls in the office asked me, "Did you get the envelope?"

I thought I had.

"You don't know?" they asked.

"I got all of the other envelopes from Rodica."

The cashier had about fifty people helping distribute the money each payday to the five thousand employees. Rodica was one of them.

"Which bills were in it?"

I explained, "Twenty-eight hundreds, one fifty, one twenty-five, and one five." The bills were always in the highest denominations.

"Did you see the money?" they asked me.

"I'm not sure."

I emptied my desk. The other girls in the office searched through their desks. We looked through all file records in our four huge closets. A policeman even came, subjecting each of us to a body search. It was awful. Rodica, the lady who had to have given me the money, emptied her desk. Nothing.

In the end, nobody felt like drinking the liquor I had bought.

People in the factory were very compassionate. They were talking of contributing five, ten, twenty-five lei or whatever they could to help me pay the debt. I thought I would take a loan from CAR to pay it off. I went home in a very sombre mood.

The next day, Rodica and her boss came to our office.

"I'll be damned," Rodica said. "You won't believe it! I'm so sorry!" She had put the envelope in the top drawer, and then a bunch of other papers had slid onto it, pushing the envelope behind the drawer, next to the back wall of her desk. In searching her office, she had taken out the drawer, but didn't think to look inside. I believed her. She was an honest girl. In all the years we worked together, we'd never had any trouble.

Now, remember? That was my birthday. After the envelope with the money was found, I told the ladies in my office that I would never serve liquor!

I always spent and served more than they gave me—chocolates, oranges, coffee, cola, etc. I didn't want to be cheap and I wanted to make up for their sweet drink. All of those items were a luxury, very expensive and very hard to get. One kilogram of coffee was worth a thousand lei, and the average monthly wage was only 1500 to 2500 lei. If bananas were imported, they were as green as lime fruits. You had to wait ages for them to ripen. *If* you had one five years ago, you had forgotten what it tasted like. I longed for the day when I could buy those items freely. I knew a day like that would come.

I Will GET OUT

12

I keep saying that I dreamed this or that. You might say that I'm a dreamer, but can you control what you dream? I can't. Praying to God about the men in my life, I felt guided through dreams. There were a lot of guys! Even the fact that there were so many was an answer to prayer of some sort—just not the answer I wanted. But I felt like God was saying, "There's nothing wrong with you as a person, but you still have to wait." How long? Why? I wanted just one man—the right one. Was he not in Romania? Throughout the years, I had a few dreams that led me to believe I would leave my country. When? How? I didn't know.

In one particular dream, I was in an old and dilapidated room, very disorderly. It was full of stuff all piled up in the centre and against the walls. There was just a small path on which to walk around. It was complete disorder. There was no paint, not even mortar on the walls. Never had I seen such a rundown room in real life. It seemed like I was looking for my shoes when a neighbour said to me, "Don't you know that your shoes are outside? They've been there for more than two months!" I thought that this room represented Romania, once a rich and beautiful country now in a state beyond description.

In another dream, it seemed like I was walking away from a valley that had a coal mine. Because of the coal dust, everything was grey—all the houses, even the laundry on the line was grey. There was no other colour in that place. It didn't matter how much you tried to keep it clean, everything would be grey after a very short time. It seemed like I was leaving this dirty place and walking between beautiful green hills, going up a path.

In yet another dream, I was in an elevator that took me from a very low level to a very high level in two seconds! In an instant!

I worked in a place that produced hundreds of articles of clothing. To prevent thefts, there were doorkeepers or porters who conducted body searches on all workers when they left work. The workers were mostly women who used sewing machines to make t-shirts, underwear, etc. One of the porter's name was Fiona, a mean woman who was hated by everybody. On any given shift change, hundreds of women would be waiting to go out through the factory gates, especially when Fiona was on duty, because she overdid her job.

In one of my dreams, Fiona was watching a small line-up of people who were getting out very fast. She had her hands on her hips and was doing nothing! Only in a dream could that be possible. I was one of those who got out unchecked by her.

One of the most significant dreams I had guided me in the way I eventually escaped from Romania. In the dream, I was by the Danube River, which formed the border between Romania and Yugoslavia for a few hundred kilometres. That wide and fast-flowing river claimed many lives. About eight or ten of us stood on a log which was flat to the ground. An instructor was coaching us: "You reach out, grab a tree and step on a log, then grab the next tree and step on the next log, and so on." Unlike in real life, there were thick trees growing in the Danube River right across. By every standing tree there was a log you could step on. That was the dream.

I cannot say that I was desperate to get out of Romania. I had no way to compare life there with another country. I didn't know any better. We only heard wonderful things about America and the free world. It was kind of like, "Oh, wouldn't it be nice if we could go there!" Just like in Joseph's dreams from the Bible, my dreams reinforced in me a certainty that a time would come when things would happen. They made me believe that there would be hope for me in the future. I was just waiting for Prince Charming to show up. It seemed like he was very slow.

In December 1983, twelve long years after my short marriage, two people were getting ready to come into my life.

WHO IS *Prince* CHARMING?

13

Mary was born in Simbateni, a village fifteen kilometres away from Arad, where I was born. On Wednesday, December 7, 1983, she said to me, "Why don't you come to my house next Tuesday? I want you to meet a new friend, Petrisor Stancu. He's from my village, a fine man. Who knows? He might be the one." She really wanted to help me find the right man.

"Oh, I don't know," I said. "This Petrisor of yours seems so far away. But I will come."

The very next day, I received a letter in the mail from Las Vegas, Nevada. To receive a letter from America was a very big deal. Who did I know there? As soon as I opened the envelope, I looked to see who had sent it.

It was John Pater, my ex-husband!

I was extremely shocked! After twelve years, he was writing to me? From America?

I still have the letter. It said:

> Lidia,
>
> I hope that this letter finds you and your family well. Please forgive me for daring to write to you, but God, who I ran away from eleven years ago, is my witness and I've had no rest for the last two and a half years. I'm tormented by dreams and constant turmoil.
>
> Lidia, I ask your forgiveness for all the trouble I've caused you. I did so many things that I'm embarrassed to face today. I realize the full extent of the pain I caused you.
>
> If you're married now, I pray that the Lord Jesus will bless your house. I remember the commitment we made before God: "Til death do us part."
>
> I'm in America on a holiday. I would say that I'm happy, but happiness left me a long time ago. There is no happiness apart from walking with Jesus. I realize now that what He has joined together, no man must separate. I'm ashamed of myself. Why did I listen to the wrong people's advice when I had the Bible for guidance? What's the use of all the riches and happiness of the moment if you lose your soul? In the name of Jesus, please forgive me.
>
> If you aren't married, if you believe God has mercy on people like me and can perform miracles in our lives, and if you believe it's possible to start a new life with Jesus and have a fresh start, please call me on Christmas Eve or New Year's Eve.

Lidia, the reason I've written these words is because I feel them from the bottom of my heart. I believe that I dream with you every day you fast. I was afraid to stand before God and face my judgment, but now I believe He has forgiven me… and that's why I have the courage to write to you today. He is good. We made a pledge before Him, and the pledge stays with us to the grave (Matthew 19).

I don't want to write too much, Lidia, but God knows our hearts. May He decide. Again, please forgive me. I wish to see you—if not here, then in eternity with Jesus.

With much respect and regret,

J. Pater

How could I express my feelings when I read that? I had very mixed emotions. First of all, it answered my question as to why I hadn't been able to marry for those twelve long years. It was as if a light came on. Then I wondered whether or not I was supposed to forgive such a man. Did God want me to forgive *him?* I thought that was asking too much. I remembered how much he had humiliated me every time I went to talk to him. How much he had made me cry! He had been so cruel, so rude, pretending to make peace when he was just playing a game. I didn't think I could forgive him. I didn't want to forgive him! I wanted revenge! *If* he came back on his hands and knees, it would have been my pleasure to crush his skull, just as he had crushed my heart.

Oh God, what should I do?

But his letter seemed so sincere! For him to say he was sorry and ask for forgiveness meant he had undergone a huge change. He had never used those words before. Never! This wasn't the man I knew. Had he really changed? Did he really want me to forgive him? Maybe he had some hidden agenda. But what? Could I trust him? Should I trust him? I didn't know if I could. What was I supposed to do?

There was a very popular song on the radio at the time, sung by Mirabela Dauer, called "Ioane, Ioane." For the rest of the week, I woke up at three or four o'clock every morning with that song ringing in my ears. I couldn't sleep because of John, just like the song said! Had I been waiting for *him* all these years? If I had known that, I wouldn't have been faithful to him. He didn't deserve my loyalty. How about Nona and their kid? Would I have to fight her all over again? And for who? The one who had mocked and betrayed me?

I also knew that no man could change my ex-husband. Only God could. This must have been the work of God. I had expected Prince Charming and what had I gotten? My ex-husband! What a twist! I'd said that I would accept whoever God wanted me to marry, even if I didn't like him… but my ex? Wasn't that too much? Wasn't there anybody else? But if God had changed him, it must have been for a reason. Maybe I had to forgive and follow him. But we were divorced! How could I? I had to escape! But leaving the country was so dangerous. Many people died or ended up in jail. Oh, what a headache!

Everybody was shocked by John's letter—my parents, Mary, my neighbours, people from work, and people from church. I thought that if my mom and Mary accepted him, it must be the will of God. People had different opinions. The girls in the office said, "Don't believe him. Don't be stupid. You can write anything on a piece of paper!" But then I gave them the letter. One by one they each read it, and one by one they said, "Yeah, maybe. He seems so genuine!"

On Tuesday, Mary reminded me, "You have to come to my

house today to meet Petrisor. I have to tell you, though, that many people have tried to acquaint him with other women. For some reason, he never seems interested. Nobody knows why. Maybe he's impotent. Who knows? I just want to tell you, don't feel bad if he shows no interest in you."

I'd had the letter from my ex for five days. I kept reading and reading and reading it. I was beginning to get used to the idea that I should go back to him.

By the time I met Petrisor, I had to tell him, "Last Thursday, I received a letter from my ex-husband. He wants me to go back to him. Although I'm not a hundred percent sure about that, I think I will. I came here today because I promised Mary and Mihai that I would come. I'm sorry."

Partly, it was my defence mechanism kicking in, just in case the guy didn't like me. On the other hand, if God wanted me to forgive John, I felt I should be upfront. Petrisor left early to catch the train home, since he was still living in his village. When he left, he told Mary and Mihai by the door, "Too bad she wants to go. I would've really liked her."

When I heard that, I smiled. Too bad!

I had another week or so to think about it before calling John. There was no internet, no Skype, none of the technology we have nowadays. I just had to wait for Christmas Eve to call him over the phone.

A couple of days before Christmas Eve, I met a lady from the church who was about my mom's age. "How are you doing?" she asked. "I recently saw that woman who went with your husband. She told me that she's going to him in Canada. Did you know about that?"

"No!" I said. I didn't tell her that John had written to me.

Her news crushed me. Nona was going to him? Did he know about that? Maybe he was just playing with me again.

Maybe he just needed something and was trying to use me. A flood of thoughts overwhelmed me. Why should I go to him? Why should I even try? What should I believe? What was the right thing to do?

By the time Christmas Eve came, I decided that I wouldn't go to him. I was very upset when I called up the number John had given me. Somebody on the line answered in Romanian.

"Tell John that he's caused me a lot of trouble," I said. "I'm not going to him. He's dead to me. Tell him to never call me again!"

John hadn't even made it home in time from his holiday to talk to me. That said, neither of us were aware of the nine-hour time delay. John had had it in his heart that if I just called, no matter what I said, it meant we would be together, so he continued to write me letters. I still have the ones he wrote in January, February, March, and April of 1984. He also started to call me every Thursday morning.

When Petrisor heard that I wasn't going to Canada, he came to me right away. He told me that he liked me a lot and that he wanted us to be together. I was caught between the two of them. Petrisor was really nice to me; he brought flowers by the bucket and wanted to please me in every way. He wanted to update his wardrobe and he wanted me to go shopping with him so that he would buy what I liked him to wear. I hadn't expected that, but he insisted.

John, on the other hand, called every week. He wanted not just any answer, but an affirmative one. I didn't know why I had to choose between the two of them. I asked pastors, elders, board members, anybody… what should I do? My pastor said that he remembered how stubborn John was. No matter how many times people had tried to convince him to reconcile, he had never agreed.

"I don't advise you to go back to him," he said. "I don't know if you can trust him."

The pastor had two daughters, both a little younger than me, so I guess he was thinking like a father.

Others were evasive and didn't know what to say. But no matter what people thought or said, I had to decide. I would have to live with that decision for the rest of my life.

Weighing THE OPTIONS

14

When John first wrote me that letter, he didn't know if I was alive or dead, if I was a hundred kilograms or three hundred, if I was married or if I had kids. He'd left Romania in August 1980 feeling that his life was unbearable. John hadn't known how to fix all the problems in his life and so he'd wanted to run away to a place where nobody could find him and he could never come back. He knew that he had ruined his life, his relationship with God, and his relationship with me. Only God could fix that mess. John couldn't face God or anyone else and felt that his life was beyond repair. In time, he got deeper and deeper into the mire and felt that it was impossible to regain his dignity.

John went to church sometimes, but he couldn't look anyone in the eye; he looked down all the time, so convicted. As soon as the preacher finished, he would shoot out the door. He was afraid that a preacher might say to him that since he had gotten involved with Nona, he would have to live with her for the rest of his life. He didn't want that. He didn't think that I would take him back, so he didn't even try. Sin took him further than he wanted to go and cost him more than he wanted to pay.

Even though he had an idea of how dangerous it was to leave the country, he knew he had to do something. With another fellow who wanted to go to West Germany, they tried and succeeded at getting out of Romania, which was no small accomplishment. On April 1, 1981, he arrived in Canada and started working right away. Like he'd said in the letter, for two and half years he had time to clear his head and think through his life. He wanted to make things right with God, and he wanted to do God's will.

The reason he didn't write to me right away was because he felt in his heart that he had wronged me deeply, and he said so in the following letters: "I always felt that I was a tyrant in the way I treated you, and you didn't deserve that." He wanted to go back to where he had started to do wrong and correct it. Very often, he dreamed that he was in my parents' backyard.

He had other dreams, too, like the one where he had a box like no other in this world. He took it apart, and then he searched the whole world and couldn't find another box like his. He went home and put his box together again. In another dream, he had a nice picture of himself that somehow ended up in the garbage. He took it out, wiped it clean, and put it in a frame.

I didn't know most of this at the time. It was just that his letters were so pleading—as was his voice on the phone. But I had heard of quite a few women from Romania who followed their husbands into the free world, only to find out that they had started other relationships. Some of these husbands then said, "I just wanted to do you a favour and help you get out of Romania, but I won't stay with you." Just imagine that you followed your husband somewhere—to Paraguay, to Mongolia, or to some other place on Earth—only to hear that. You don't know anyone, you don't know the language... well, what do you do? A fine lady who followed her husband to Canada used to say to John, "John, all men are pigs!" Her adult son would laugh and say to her, "Mom, but John is a man, too!"

Given my previous experiences with him, it was very difficult to make the right decision. Being with John meant that I had to forgive and forget. I had to swallow a lot of hurt and pride. Simple words like "mushrooms" or "bricks" still brought back very painful memories. Could I do that for the rest of my life?

Now I had Petrisor to think about, too. He was an engineer, a very smart man. He had finished university with the highest mark possible, yet he was modest and humbly dressed. He became very attached to me. He was about twelve years older than me, but he was still good-looking, witty, and very kind. He never lied to me. He loved to take pictures of me with flowers or tree blossoms in the background.

Every Thursday when Petrisor came over, I had this dreamy look on my face. From that look, he knew right away that John had called again. He thought that I must still love John very much and that I couldn't give up on him. It wasn't love that made me think of John, though; it was the nagging feeling that God wanted me to go back to my ex-husband. Petrisor couldn't quite get that. He wanted me to forget about John. He brought me an audio tape with a very lovely song on it by

Angela Similea, a beautiful and talented singer. The message of the song was that you cannot live your life from memories, even if you regret a lost ideal. It was a lovely song!

Another good thing about Petrisor was that he was willing to help me in everything I had to do. One day I told him, "You better go home early today, because I need to lay down a bit. I have my period, then I need to wash the windows."

"Just lay down and I'll wash them for you."

Right away, I remembered that when I had been married to John, I got sick and went to the hospital for a few days. My mom was washing windows and John said to her, "Don't wash them! Wait for Lidia to come home from the hospital and she'll do them." Thankfully, my mom washed them anyway.

I didn't think that I had any guidance from God in going for either one of them. I felt that God had left me on my own and I was wavering, not sure who I should choose. I would have rather gone for Petrisor. He was kind, I didn't have any bad memories of him, and it seemed much simpler. In restoring my relationship with John, there was a lot of baggage, bad memories, uncertainty of the future, plus complications with his mistress and their child. It might have been good to reconcile with him and correct all wrongs, to continue to be a family and walk forward. However, I wasn't sure I could go down that road.

I leaned toward Petrisor, until Mary gave me a good scare about that relationship.

"I have some bad news for you," Mary said to me one day.

"What is it?"

"It looks like Petrisor is going to marry an eye doctor."

This surprised me. "What are you talking about? Who told you that?"

"I visited my mom in the village yesterday," Mary said. "Her neighbours, two old women, went to the eye doctor in Arad.

The lady doctor asked about Petrisor and how he is, among other things. They think he's going to marry her."

I went home devastated. I called him at his work and left a message for him to come to my house. I then prostrated myself before God, praying and crying and not understanding why this man had left me without even saying a word. I was crushed beyond belief.

When he came, I saw that he was in a very good mood. I didn't know what to believe and what to say. Finally, I told him what I had heard.

"How can you believe that? Old wives tales!" he said. "That lady grew up in a very poor family in our village. Her father died and her mom was left with three small children. My parents helped that family and looked after her, even helping her become a doctor. She's like a sister to me. If I wanted to marry her, I would've done so a long time ago. She's not for me and I'm not for her. End of story. There's nothing between us. And while we're on the topic, I should tell you that some years ago I dated Brother Jurjeu's daughter. But I saw that she was making a fuss and I left her. There was nothing between me and her, either."

Now, Brother Jurjeu was to me just as big as the Apostle Paul from the Bible. He was a very lean man, close to seventy years old, with a deep, rich voice. He had planted a lot of churches in many villages around Arad. For Petrisor to say that he had dated Brother Jurjeu's daughter was a big claim. Much sooner than I expected, I had to check up on that piece of information. Some big revelations were in store for me.

I Have DECIDED

15

After receiving John's other letters, and after talking to him on the phone, he convinced me that it was God's will for me to go back to him.

Knowing that Petrisor was a good guy, and wanting to make it up to him, I decided to introduce him to one of my girlfriends, Miruna. She was delighted and was waiting for him to show up at her door.

When I told Petrisor that again I had decided to go to John, he was devastated. He almost started crying. I felt really sorry for him. Right away, he proceeded to tell me everything about himself, that throughout his life he had lived with ten different women; he even mentioned one name I knew. If I wanted, he would give me all the details. I couldn't believe that such a lovely lady I knew from the church had lived with him! I told him that I didn't want to know about his past and that, if he didn't mind, I had a really good friend who was single and wanted to meet him.

"If you don't want me, don't pass me on to somebody else, because I'm not interested," he said. "In my entire life, I've never been more attracted to a woman than I am to you. Many friends and neighbours have introduced me to women, but I had no interest in them. I'm so sorry that I didn't meet you twenty years ago."

He told me that he would rather die than not be with me. *Yeah, right!* I thought. *Cheap talk!*

Later on, though, he proved it. At the time, the situation was heartbreaking. I really didn't know what was best.

Not long after that, while in church, I saw John and Nona's son coming towards me with a little piece of paper. On it he had written that I should leave his daddy alone, because he wanted to go to his dad with his mom. That same week, I received a letter from Nona telling me the same thing: she wanted to go to him and they had gotten married through the Canadian Embassy (which I knew was a lie). When I read her letter, I became furious and started shaking.

I decided to reply to her letter:

> Do you have the audacity to tell me that I'm breaking up your family when I know for certain that you two aren't even married? Did you forget what you told me long ago, when we were married, that you liked, loved, and wanted my husband? How dare you do that? Have you no shame?

I went to bed thinking that I would mail the letter the next day. That night, I dreamed that I had an ink smudge at the corner of my mouth. I decided that I wouldn't lower myself to her level. I never sent it.

I also heard that she had gone to the church board meetings and told them that I was interfering with and breaking up her family. One of the board members, who had prayed years earlier with John and me for our reconciliation, said, "Lidia must be excommunicated!"

When I heard that, my heart broke. My beloved church, which meant so much to me! I called John and told him that the church wanted to kick me out if I went back to him. I also told him the whole story with Nona.

He said the church wasn't right to do that. "Don't you remember? It was the church that crucified Christ!"

I was amazed at how smart he was, how he knew just what to say to comfort me. I told him that I didn't want to fight anyone for him and that it would be better if he took Nona back. Besides, they had a child together. He said that he had left behind a fifty-thousand-lei apartment in the child's name, plus furniture and amenities worth twenty thousand lei.

"You're my wife," he said, "and we should be together."

Nevertheless, I felt too tired to start a battle for him. I told him that I wanted to try marrying my friend from Romania.

I wrote a short letter to Petrisor, letting him know that I had given up on going to Canada, and if he wanted we could continue our friendship. That evening, he had a terrible toothache. He would read my letter and his toothache would subside for a while, so great was his joy. He read it twenty times that night.

Petrisor again started coming to my house. Miruna was still waiting for him, though, and I knew that if I told her he had come back to me, I would be a hypocrite. If I didn't, I would be a hypocrite as well. So I decided to tell her. I felt bad, but what else could I do?

No doubt, Miruna was very disappointed.

Consequently, she started telling me that she had heard Petrisor had dated Brother Jurjeu's daughter and that Jurjeu had said he would never allow his daughter to marry such a man. She kept saying that I should call Jurjeu and ask him about Petrisor.

"He told me about dating that girl," I said to her, "and he never lies to me."

But she pestered me so much that I agreed to look into it. I called Brother Jurjeu, who was from another Baptist church from Arad. He didn't know me, but I had heard him preach and knew what he looked like. When he answered the phone, I told him that I was a young woman from the church of Sperantza, that I was dating Petrisor, and that I'd heard he knew him. I asked his opinion about Petrisor.

"My opinion about him is very good," he said.

"Good?" I asked.

"Yes, excellent."

"Excellent?"

Miruna, who was in the room with me, sank lower and lower in her armchair.

"Yes," Brother Jurjeu continued. "He dated my daughter some years ago."

"But then why—"

"Why didn't he marry her?" he asked, completing my thought.

"Yes."

"Simply, because he didn't ask for her. He is an excellent man. I know his father, too, truly a very good believer. About that time, another young man came and in four days he asked for my daughter in marriage, so now he's my son-in-law. A very fine man, too."

"By the way, I have one more question," I said, deciding to ask his opinion on my other matter. "I separated from my husband many years ago. He lived with another woman and then escaped to Canada. Now he wants to reconcile with me, but I don't know if I should do it, because they have a child together."

"Even if they have ten children, you must go back to your husband!" he said very firmly. "There is no question about it! Petrisor is a very good guy, I know him, but you have to go back to your husband!"

His tone dispelled all my doubts. Nobody had answered my question with such assurance and authority.

"I will talk to a board of elders that comes from a few different churches," Jurjeu continued. "I will present your case without telling them your name. All of them are godly people who deal with very difficult cases. Call me back in a month and I'll tell you what they said."

I did call back, a month later, and he confirmed everything he had said the first time. All the elders had agreed that reconciliation was the right thing to do.

"When you and John got married," he explained, "you gave your pledge to God and to each other, becoming a family. When you separated, that bond was broken, and as a consequence other things have happened. If you really want to do God's will, you both have to go back to that point in time and repent before God. Repair your relationship with God and with each other."

What he said made sense. But that was a lot easier said than done.

He was the only voice in Romania telling me beyond the shadow of a doubt that I must go back to my ex-husband—no ifs, ands, or buts.

In April 1984, on the Saturday before Easter, a family from Canada came to our house. It was Mike and Alice Putici from Taber, a community close to Lethbridge where John was living. They were about my parents' age and, being of Romanian descent, were visiting relatives near Arad. They knew John from the church in Lethbridge.

John had asked them to come by my house and try to convince me to go back to him. I remember that I was in the middle of spring cleaning when they came. I was fasting that day. I served them a short and strong coffee. In Romania, the more important the guests, the stronger the coffee. They tasted it but couldn't drink it!

Mike and Alice told me how good John was. He was a very hard worker, he owned his own house, and he really had changed.

"Just come and see," they said. "If you don't like it, you can come back."

I don't know if they realised that it was impossible to do that. As a Romanian, you could not get out of Romania. I told them that I had considered travelling to Canada, but it was too complicated. I wasn't sure about my future with him, so I had decided to stay in Romania where I had met a very good guy. They insisted, but I told them I had made up my mind that I didn't want to go.

"It's too bad that you don't want to come," Alice said. "You are a beautiful wife." She said *wife*—not woman.

Mary suggested that I go to Oradea and attend a very large church north of Arad. She insisted that I go one Sunday and ask that pastor his opinion. I did just that, and at the end of the service I spoke with the pastor. When he heard my case, he said, "Dear sister, it is up to you. If you want, you can go to your ex-husband, or if you want you can marry the guy from here. It is according to the Bible any way you want to do it."

He didn't shine any light to our case. I was back to square one, according to him. I left crying.

Here, I have to give credit to Florica, my sister-in-law. She comforted me and told me not to cry, because God knows all our sorrows and He doesn't leave us alone. She was right. Mary was also disappointed when she heard what the pastor had told me.

I kept calling Jurjeu every month. When he heard what the other pastor had said, he replied, "That pastor is young. He doesn't have the life experience of these elders, and he just doesn't know enough." Indeed, that pastor was young—roughly my age.

I suddenly felt that everybody was against me. Twelve years ago, I had prayed with a lot of board members for John to come back. Now that the answer to my prayer had come, they didn't recognized it as such, but instead ostracized me. One of the board members, wanted to expel me from the church. It seemed as though Nona was winning again. It was so unfair, so unjust!

What had I done? All those years, I had tried to do the right thing and now I was in the wrong again, no matter what I did. They didn't kick me out of the church, but there was a lot of pressure around me.

So I prayed. "Lord God Almighty from heaven, if it's true that John is really changed by You, and if he's prompted by You, Lord, to come back to me, then You have to fight for me. You have to untangle this mess, because I can't fight anymore. If all this is true, then Lord, You have to show me, in a powerful way. And You have to carry out this reconciliation between us, because I can't do it."

I had to leave it all with God. There was nothing else I could do. I didn't feel like going to church anymore. Not to my church, anyway.

I felt cast out.

I felt like a black sheep.

Yet I had no idea how powerful and painful the answer to my prayer would be.

Palm SUNDAY

16

Petrisor loved me like his own soul. We would go on picnics out in the nature. He loved to take pictures of flowers or fruit tree blossoms—or of me. He told me jokes. Sometimes he brought his eighty-four-year-old father to our house; his mother had passed on some ten years earlier. His parents had one daughter who had died of tuberculosis when she was seventeen years old. Then they had a little boy who died at eleven months. Then they had Petrisor. Both father and son loved and respected each other very much.

On Sunday afternoons, we would all sit in our house talking. One day, the topic of baptism came up and we found out with consternation that the old man didn't believe in baptism. It was shocking! He was saying something about a comma by the word baptism in some verse in the Bible, and according to him you didn't need to be baptised. That's when I realized that neither one of them were baptised. I believe that I spoke very confidently that baptism, along with faith, was the requirement for being saved. If God required from Adam and Eve just a simple act of obedience, wouldn't He require the same from us? They disobeyed in one way, we disobeyed in another. All my life, I'd heard and believed the verse that says,

> Go into all the world and preach the good news to all creation. Whoever believes *and is baptized* will be saved, but whoever does not believe will be condemned. (Mark 16:16, emphasis mine)

To me, it was very clear. It was a simple act of obedience. Also, I considered the reverse logic to be true: you didn't get baptised because you didn't believe.

I pondered that and wondered if I had been taught wrong. I didn't think so, but I prayed earnestly and sincerely about it.

You wouldn't be surprised to learn that I had a dream about Petrisor's father; in my dream, he had glaucoma. To me, that was enough. Glaucoma was a disease of the eye that progressed to blindness. In my view, he was headed for spiritual blindness.

"Why would God listen to your requests when you pray?" I asked Petrisor. "God had one request of you and you neglected it."

Even though I would have preferred that he get baptised, I didn't put that condition on him. Baptism was a personal act of obedience to God. Knowing how much Petrisor strived to please me in even the smallest thing, I didn't think it would be an issue. But it was an issue with his father. Petrisor's stance was that he would obey his father as long as his father was alive. Then he would get baptised.

That turn of events put a damper on our relationship. Petrisor stopped coming to our house. He would come to church, but leave before I could talk to him. Perhaps his father had told him not to come to me, or maybe he just did it in deference to his father. He was torn in two by his love for his father and for me.

Two weeks passed, then four. Six. Nothing.

If you don't come to me, I certainly won't chase after you, I thought.

My life was stalled again. I couldn't believe it! I had given up on my ex-husband for him and now he was nowhere. What was happening?

I felt like there was a thick black velvet curtain in front of my eyes. I really wanted to pull it aside to know what was beyond. Like usual, I sent an emergency call to God and I fasted ten days.

I was called one day to go to the hospital. Petrisor had a cold that wouldn't go away. He told me that he had been digging out a root cellar in the yard by hand. He had put all his frustrations into the work and sweated heavily without stopping. His voice got really raspy and he ran a high fever. They did some tests. A month later, in January 1985, we found out that he had cancer of the thyroid gland.

I went through a horrible phase. January, February, March... I kept crying, crying, crying. I couldn't stop. I felt guilty and I didn't know why. He became weaker and weaker. The man I wanted to marry was dying. He couldn't lie down in bed, he felt he couldn't breathe, and he tried to sleep sitting in a chair with his head on the table. His whole body swelled up beyond recognition for two weeks. He had no strength left at all and was taking morphine. The cancer had spread down from his neck to his lungs.

"I will have a horrible death," he told me. "I will asphyxiate."

Someone else advised me that he would have an easy death, that he would just go out like a candle, but I found it very difficult to tell Petrisor that—and I didn't, because I wasn't sure if it was true.

Petrisor was a good man, and he never smoke or drank. There were some stages in his sickness that I won't describe. He always wanted me to stay with him. He felt that his disease was easier for him when I was around.

On Friday, April 5, 1985, just before Palm Sunday, he died in his sleep at 3:00 in the morning. Sadly, neither he nor his father ended up getting baptised.

The next day, my sister-in-law from Germany came with me to his house; she tried to comfort me and his father. The funeral was on Palm Sunday.

I didn't have any intimate relationships with him or anybody else. I had wanted to save that until we were married.

For the funeral, I wore a white-knitted outfit from Germany with a big, navy blue corsage, a large dark flower pinned on the top of my outfit. When the funeral was over, I noticed going home that I had lost my flower somewhere in the cemetery.

That week, between Palm and Easter Sunday, was one the most painful periods of my life. There are a lot of fruit trees in Romania, and they all bloomed that week. It was so beautiful, yet so painful for my heart. Petrisor had loved to take exquisite pictures of flowers and blossoms, but now he was gone. To me it seemed like all that beauty was getting its sap from him who was underground.

His eighty-five-year-old father was left alone. He offered to give me Petrisor's house and car, but I declined. He kept saying, "Three children and all three of them in a good place." Later, on Petrisor's funeral stone, it was written: "Goodbye Father and Lidia." I wished that my name wasn't there, but I didn't have the heart to say that to a broken old man. I wanted so much to know about him and where he was. All that week, I cried as I went to work and back.

On the Friday after his burial, I had a dream. The village doctor who had treated Petrisor, a lady by the name of Violet, a woman I'd never met, called me and said, "Lidia, do you know what the angel said?"

"No," I replied.

"The angel said, 'Do not try to get through eternity's gate!'"

I thought that she wanted to scold me for something. "I didn't mean any harm."

"That is excluded," she said.

From that dream, I understood that nobody was accusing me of anything and that I shouldn't try to find out where he was. I understood that I had to let go of him and go on living. God had taken him away and there was nothing we could do about it.

When I talked again to Brother Jurjeu, I told him that Petrisor had died.

"Didn't I tell you?" Jurjeu said. "You have to go back to your husband. Even if you would've married him, you would've changed your name, but your problem would still be the same. And now I know why Petrisor didn't marry my daughter! He had a short life."

Two months later, in June 1985, I went to the Black Sea for a vacation. It was raining all the time, just like in my soul.

I understood that I had to go back to my husband. God had showed me that in a very powerful and painful way. My answer to God was, "Lord, if You want me to, I will go back to my ex-husband, but if it doesn't work, I wash my hands of it."

I called John on the phone and told him that Petrisor had died, that I had nobody in my life.

Petrisor had once brought me the Angela Similea song, about memory, hoping it would help me forget about John. The irony of it was that the same song now worked against Petrisor. I couldn't sustain myself from the memories alone; I had to go on living.

JUST *Give*

ME A SECOND CHANCE

17

Maria, John's sister, was married and had two beautiful children, a sweet little girl named Simona and a son named Valentin. Her husband's name was Traian. They lived in the village of Covasant, some thirty-five kilometres east of Arad. Maria's whole family was excited that John was trying to come back to me.

After many years, I decided to visit Maria and reconnect with her family. Maria was pregnant and her husband said, "If it's a girl, we're going to name her Lidia. If it's a boy, I don't know, maybe John." They were gentle and understanding with me… and they didn't push me to go back to John.

John's mother was also happy about the possibility of reconciliation. His father and younger brother had passed away, but they would've been thrilled along with the rest of the family.

When I talked to John in June 1985, he told me that he would be gone from 6:00 a.m. to 9:00 p.m. seven days a week, working road construction far from his house. There were no phones close to his workplace. He would be gone the whole summer and he wanted to rent out his house to a woman.

"Don't!" I told him. "If you love me, don't rent it out to anybody. Forget about the money. My peace of mind is worth more than that money."

He didn't rent the house. He also said that he would try to come to Romania by November 1, when the work season was over.

John had become a Canadian citizen and had applied for a visa to the Romanian Embassy in Toronto. He wanted to visit Romania and reconnect with me. If he came as a Canadian citizen, he would be safe in Romania, because all foreign citizens were treated very well. Otherwise he could've ended up in jail. On the way, he stopped in Germany and visited with my brother Avram, his wife Aurica, and their lovely four-year-old daughter Gloria. They were very supportive of our reconciliation. They even let John use their Mercedes to drive to Romania.

John was supposed to arrive in Romania around November 1, 1985. It had been many years since I had last seen him, so when the day came I was jittery and didn't know what to expect. All day, I was edgy and restless.

Time passed, and he didn't come. Maybe there had been a big line-up at the border and he was delayed. It happened often.

The second day was a little easier, but he still didn't show up.

Maybe tomorrow he'll come, I thought.

He didn't.

The next day, I wondered what was happening and whether or not he was coming at all. By the fifth day, I concluded that he had probably changed his mind. On the sixth day, I was relaxed; it seemed like he wasn't coming anymore.

At 5:00 on the morning of November 7, a Thursday, my mom woke me up: "John's coming right now! He called me from downtown. He'll be here in five minutes."

When I heard that, I got the runs! All the emotions from the week had drained me. I barely had time to calm down.

Then I saw him. He had on a short leather jacket. He stretched out his hand to shake mine, but I pretended not to see it. I wasn't sure what was going to happen and how well this was going to work. He looked pale and had gotten a perm in his hair. He was calm and attentive.

Soon I had to go to work. He offered to give me a ride.

I'm more entitled to that car than he is, because it is my brother's, I thought.

While we were in the car, he said, "Just give me a second chance! I know I don't deserve it, and I don't expect you to make up your mind right away. But please, give me a second chance. That's all I ask. I'll be waiting for you when you get off work."

He did wait for me, and then we drove to his sister's home in Covasant. While there, he spoke to Traian and his father; I was with Maria and her mother-in-law. Maria knew that I was trying to get my driver's licence and asked me how the test had gone.

"It was postponed!" John said, jumping into the discussion. I had actually failed the test, which he knew, because I had just told him on the drive over. I was surprised to see how quick he was to protect me. Even though he was in the men's group, his ears were tuned to where I was and what we were talking about.

Oh, he's a lot better than I remember, I thought with delight. *He's not acting at all like the John I once knew.* He was humble and ready to cooperate. It sounded good!

Day after day, he drove me to work and picked me up afterwards. I was so glad for the change I saw in him. It was unbelievable! That had been on my prayer list, to have a man who loved me, who was kind and respected, and who appreciated me. The Lord had been listening after all!

That month, we tried to get reacquainted with each other.

I became very attached to him, but I still didn't go to bed with him. There were a lot of quirks that needed to be worked out. For instance, I wondered if we had to get remarried in the church after remarrying legally. To find out the answer, I spoke to Ritza, an older lady from our church. When she was young, she had left her husband and went with a bum who beat her up and treated her like dirt. They'd had a child together. She had been smart enough to realize her mistake, divorced the bum, and then remarried her husband, who was a fine and very good man to accept her back as well as the kid. I asked her if she had gotten remarried in the church.

"No," she told me. "I didn't have to. In our case, I was the culprit, but he was kind enough to take me back. We were married in the church the first time. Before God, we were still married."

We had a really good time with my brother's car. Thank you, Avram and Aurica! Twenty-five years later, we found out that the police in Romania had kept a close eye on John because he'd been driving a car from West Germany and he was a Canadian citizen. In 2011, John's cousin told us that in 1986, when he had gone to the army, the colonel asked him, "Who is that guy with the Mercedes? How is he related to you? We know his every move!"

The police knew where we went and how long we stayed. They were watching us constantly. In fact, one policeman stopped us on the way to Timisoara and went around the car, trying to find something wrong so he could give us a fine. He found nothing, so he asked for a pack of Kent cigarettes, which were one hundred lei a pack. You could only buy them in shops for foreigners. The following week, he stopped us again and we gave him the Kent which we had bought for him.

We visited friends and relatives and tried to get an idea of how I could get out of Romania. People tried to escape into Yugoslavia, the neighbouring country to the west. Yugoslavia had a totally different policy than Romania. Their people could go anywhere they wished and return home without political consequence. They had a refugee camp where men would try to get to, if they could escape from Romania, Czechoslovakia, Poland, or Albania. Once in a refugee camp, they would apply to go to West Germany, the United States, Canada, or Australia, if they could find sponsors. John had opened a file and sponsored me as a fiancée at the Canadian Embassy in Beograd in January 1984, when he had first convinced me to go back to him. He had kept the file, even when I'd changed my mind two months later.

John had bought a small house in Canada, which was paid off because he'd worked hard and saved his money. He was ready to sell the house and pay somebody to take me out of Romania. He didn't want to put his skin on the line to do that; he knew how risky it was. There were guides who offered to take you to the border in exchange for thousands of lei, but it was no guarantee. Some people who did get out of the country were handcuffed by the Yugoslavian authorities and sent back, where they were beaten half to death and sent to jail for a few years. People who went to jail in Romania were treated very roughly.

You didn't want to be there. There was no guarantee you would get out alive.

The rumour was that eighty percent of the people who escaped Romania were sent back by the Yugoslavian or Serbian authorities. It was also said that the Romanian government offered a ton of salt for each person sent back from Yugoslavia (Romania was rich in salt and other minerals). It was very risky trying to get out of Romania.

November was soon gone and John's visa expired. He had to leave Romania. I could see that he had become a new man, a good man. I realized that we could be a family with God's blessing. I was sorry to see him go.

He went to Austria and visited some friends who had just escaped from Romania by crossing the Danube. An idea crossed his mind; maybe I could do that, too. I had told him about my dreams... one of my dreams had included something about crossing the Danube.

John then went to the Canadian Embassy in Beograd and told them he needed a visa for his fiancée. The counsellor said to him, "Just bring her here and we'll give her the minister's permit." He then returned to Canada and requested a second visa to visit Romania.

Trying
TO GET OUT

18

One month later, on December 31, 1985, John was back at my parents' house. In less than thirty days he had gone to Canada, obtained another visa for Romania, and returned. He told me that he had gone to a pastor in Vrset and asked for his help getting me out. The town of Vrset and Margita were positioned on the Serbian side of the border. The pastor had told him to talk to Ioca, an older and faithful believer whose land was right on the border and who spoke Romanian. Ioca did his best. He came to Romania and tried to help, but it snowed a lot and proved impossible to cross safely. We had to wait.

One of the relatives John and I visited was my cousin Dumitru, his wife Jeny, and their two little girls, Anca and

Andreea. They lived in Jebel. Dumitru's dad was my mom's younger brother. I knew that Dumitru was very interested in leaving Romania, but John didn't. Dumitru was the one who had told me earlier to leave Petrisor and go back to my ex. He had hoped John would open up the discussion about escaping. John didn't know my relatives very well, however, so he was careful; you never knew who you could trust. When John came to Romania the second time, I told him to talk to Dumitru. As soon as they knew they could talk openly, they became buddies.

They tried to find contacts, trustworthy people who could help us. My brother Costica was also very interested in leaving Romania, but his wife didn't want him to go. I didn't blame her; it was very risky, indeed. We had no car, so we had to travel by train.

All along the border were sentinel posts with guards watching constantly so that no one crossed to the other side. If they saw you crossing, they shot you. Many people tried to get to the villages close to the border to see if they could find a way to get across. What those people didn't know was that there were police checkpoints positioned on the highways within five kilometres of the border.

Let's say you and your buddy got in a car and tried to approach one of these villages. The policeman would stop you and ask, "Where are you going?"

You might say, "To Moravita."

"Why?"

"To visit my uncle."

"Who is your uncle?"

You don't really have an uncle, so you try to think fast. But he quickly figures out that you're lying.

"Where does your uncle live?"

If you don't have a certain name and address, you're caught. People would go to jail because of that. Another crime as a Romanian citizen was to have foreign currency on you, like American or Canadian dollars or German marks. You went to jail if you were caught with that.

While we were at my parents' house talking about departure plans, John would throw a pillow over the phone. I thought he was taking it too far, but if you read Ioan Pacepa's book *The Red Horizons*, you would be amazed to see how right he was. The rotary telephone was the only type of phone a Romanian could have. In the plastic body of each phone were imbedded small microphones that could pick up the dialogue in the house— *after* you hung up the phone!

The secret police later conducted an experiment to show Ceausescu that they could listen in when people spoke in their own homes. One officer dialled a random number in Bucharest.

"Hello?" the officer said.

"Yes?" a man responded.

"Is this the National Theatre?"

"No," said the man, then hung up.

Afterward they could hear the man's wife ask, "Who was that on the phone?"

"Some idiot wanting to know if this was the National Theatre. Now, put that Free Europe radio louder... I want to hear if that pig is going to China again."

The officer stopped the connection; he knew that "the pig" was a reference to Ceausescu.

My younger brother lived in West Germany, so our phone was tapped and we knew that. We had proof, too. The police had caught Dumitru in a house with other people and assumed that they were making plans to escape. They arrested Dumitru and interrogated him. One officer ordered him to go sit on another officer's desk. If he did, the second officer would say, "How dare you sit on my desk!" If he didn't, the first officer would say, "How dare you not listen to my order!" They wanted Dumitru to testify that he was making plans to escape, but he wouldn't. They made him face the wall and lift his hands up while they hit him in the kidneys with a rubber stick. That way, there wouldn't be any marks on his body. They then had him beaten on his head and the soles of his feet. The man who was supposed to do this dirty job told my cousin, "If you scream really loud, I won't hit you hard, but if you don't, I have to, or else they'll know that I don't do my job." Even though that guy was trying to be kind to him, Dumitru's face was really swollen when he got home.

The fact that he was unjustly accused and beaten made Dumitru determined to leave the country. He knew of many people who had been treated the same way.

The officers also asked Dumitru, "Why did your cousin Lidia wait for you at the train station? What did you talk to her about?"

It was true. Dumitru had called me on the phone and told me that he had to go to Oradea by train. "Why don't you come to the train station at 5:10 in the morning?" he had asked me. "That way, we can talk for the ten minutes while the train is stopped in Arad." We wanted to talk face to face, not by phone.

I remember very distinctly that I saw a police officer in the train station at 5:00 a.m. and I wondered why he was there, because the place was deserted at that time in the morning. Later on, I realized that he was probably there for us, trying to prevent us from talking. I went to the train station and talked to Dumitru, then went home while he continued his trip.

Sometimes John would go alone to Timisoara or Oradea, either by train or by hitchhiking. On two such occasions, when he was in the car with people who gave him a ride, they almost crashed to death. John felt that the car once slid off the icy highway for no reason and headed for the huge trees lining the road. Both times they were inches away from death. He felt that the devil was really after him. He worried, just like Jonah, that other people might suffer harm because of him.

On occasion, we went together to different places, trying to make arrangements for me. On Sundays, we would go to church, and in that time it seemed like the message from God to us was always the same: *Patience, patience, patience.* Whether we were in Oradea, Arad, or Timisoara, in these months all preachers spoke from Romans 5:3, emphasizing suffering, perseverance, character, and hope.

Getting READY

19

While on a moving train once, John grabbed hold of the handrail and tried to get up the steps and inside the wagon. It was also very crowded, and John could've been thrown off. Instead he sprained his wrist. It swelled up and was very painful.

Dumitru took him to an old babushka in a small village, who knew how to fix things like that.

"Where are you from?" she demanded.

"Ka–NAA–da," he replied, giving the Romanian pronunciation of Canada.

She had never heard of it. She thought it was some small hamlet off in the neck of the woods. "Why don't you go to Timisoara instead and make something of yourself? Forget about KaNAAda."

She did fix his hand and they left, thanking her and amusing themselves.

John's visa expired at the end of January 1986, but he was able to get an extension until February 20. Even that approached quickly, though, and he soon had to leave. Our problem wasn't solved yet. It seemed like everything was falling through. Nothing worked. However, through all that, we were getting closer to each other and bonding really well.

I could see how hard he was trying. He didn't want to leave any doubt that he was any less than a hundred percent for me and for "restoring the years the locusts had eaten." If he went to town and had to wait in line to buy bread or eggs, he made sure he was home in time, even if he came home without the items. It was more important for him to regain my trust than anything else.

We became more determined than ever to get out of Romania, and soon, but we hadn't yet found the right path.

He left on February 20, taking most of my clothes with him. He stopped by the Canadian Embassy in Beograd and begged them to help me get out of Romania.

"We will give her a visa to enter Canada when she comes here," he was told, "but that's all we can do."

John threatened to chain himself to the decorative post in front of the Canadian Embassy in Beograd and throw the key into traffic, starving himself until his problem was solved.

John had returned to Canada defeated twice. He felt like he really had to be prepared this third time, or else! He also realized that he couldn't pay anyone else to get me out of Romania. My husband knew that he had to do the job himself, and he had to do it right. He needed to be fully prepared and he needed God's help more than anything.

Just like he had before, he sent his passport to Toronto to gain entrance to Romania—for the third time in six months.

John knew that just praying wasn't enough. He needed to fast before God. He then fasted twenty-one days. He fasted just like I did, by eating and drinking only in the evening. He felt that it was easy to fast, because his problem was bigger than a mountain and he was really worried.

People in Canada tried to convince John that he didn't have to go back to me; there were fine girls in Canada he could marry. He didn't want to hear about that. John really wanted to follow God's will and he was afraid he might go to hell if he didn't reconcile with me, knowing how he had treated me. He really wanted to correct that.

As soon as he got his passport, he headed back to Romania. On April 2, at 6:00 a.m., he knocked on my bedroom door.

"Give me the key," he said in English.

I had started to pick up a few words in English. He had left the luggage in the street, jumped over the fence, and asked me for the key to open the door from the street. In Romania, people had high fences with metal gates and doors which were locked up at night. He brought in the luggage and handed me a package about six inches thick and about thirty inches wide.

"What is this?" I asked.

"These are the logs you dreamed about."

"But logs are long and round!"

"It's a boat," he explained. "An inflatable boat that I bought from Austria. Remember? You dreamed about crossing the Danube, and I think your dream is going to come true."

He then told me that he had spoken with people who had crossed the Danube in an area that wasn't heavily guarded by soldiers, but in order to get there we had to cross the mountains on foot.

"We tried going on dry land, and it didn't work," he said, "but I think our best chance is by boat. I could take you to the

111

route I used when I left, but you have to cross a very deep ditch full of water and then walk many days through a swamp. The mosquitoes eat you alive in there. If you catch a cold, you could get really sick, then that's it. I don't want to lose you now that I got you back!"

Before embarking on such a big adventure, we decided to go to Bucharest and try to do it legally—either have the divorce cancelled or submit papers for remarriage. We went to the Foreign Affairs Department and knocked on doors. A man in a small basement office told us that we didn't stand a chance. We heard from other people waiting in line that a woman who married a foreigner had to wait fifteen years to join her husband outside Romania.

We left knowing that we had to do it on our own; we couldn't rely on the Romanian government.

We went to a big restaurant to eat, and it was very noisy. A lot of very confident people were seated on high stools by the bar ordering food and drinks. It was a huge room full of people and I felt small and insignificant.

"You are worth more than anyone else in here," John told me. He made me feel good.

Next we went to Cismigiu Lake, where we rented a boat and enjoyed a romantic evening, gliding on the still, clear water under the willows that guarded the lake. The next day, we left Bucharest and returned home.

At times, John felt so frustrated that he'd say to me, "Just let me scream." Screaming helped relieve the pressure of not being able to solve our problem.

John and I took the train to Resita, a city in the south where we could try the boat on the lake. When we got on the train, my brother Costica was there. I was so happy to have my brother join us, and I really believed my brother would come along with me when I left Romania. We later tried to leave Romania with my brother, but unfortunately it rained! We had to postpone and wait for sunny days. It seemed like every time my brother was around, things didn't go as desired. We thought the reason was that his wife was very much against him leaving Romania. In the end, he decided to go back home. He didn't want to lose his family.

Dumitru, too, joined us in Resita. The boat worked fine. We decided to make preparations to cross the mountains on foot from a starting place called Eftimie Murgu. From that little town, we had to keep going south for eighty kilometres before hitting the Danube, which formed the border with Yugoslavia.

During that time, my mother-in-law came to our house and slept overnight. John had gone to Timisoara and came the next day. For some reason, she started telling me some gruesome things about Nona and what she had done to tie John up with witchcraft. It made such an impact on me that I told him the next day that I didn't want to go with him anymore. His face fell. He said that he would go back to Canada and never speak to his mother again.

When my mom heard me saying that, she told me not to take into consideration what my mother-in-law had said. "Don't you see that he loves you and cares for you? She told me the same things, but I didn't think she would tell you that. You can see that he's a changed man and wants to do the will of God. Not only that, but right now a few countries are involved in your case—Romania, Yugoslavia, Canada. Don't listen to her!"

I decided to let go of the hurt. I didn't want to hold that against my mother-in-law, but she wasn't wise. Praying to God, I realized that the blood of Jesus could wash away any impurity from my life, from his life, from anybody's life. I knew that the power of God was bigger than any scheme of the devil.

I decided to leave all the hurt behind and get ready for the trip of a lifetime.

Going

HIKING

20

The fact that John was hanging around for months was a pretty good clue that he might be up to something. A lot of people were looking for a safe way to get out of Romania and many of them expressed their desire to join our group. John could've had a busload of people, but we came to realize that the bigger the group, the more difficult it would be to agree on a plan. Some of them thought they were smart when in fact they were just lippy. They wouldn't dare go on their own, but they were more than willing to give us advice. We knew that the smaller the group, the better our chances of success.

It seemed like my brother was out. I remember trying to keep my mom up to date with our plans.

"Don't even tell me," she said. "I don't want to know."

I guess she trusted God and John. She knew that wherever I might be, I would be in good hands. She didn't want to be shaking in her boots for the next week or month, worrying about my safety when there was nothing she could do to help me apart from prayer. Another reason was that if—*when*—the police called and asked about where I was, my parents could swear that they didn't know anything. How right she was!

We decided that there would be only four of us in our group—John, me, Dumitru, and Florian, one of Dumitru's younger brothers. Florian didn't want to leave the country; he just came to help with the luggage and be a companion for John on his return from the Danube. My husband could only come with us to the river; then he had go back, pick up his luggage and passport, and leave through customs. He had to have the exit visa on his passport.

Dumitru's wife Jeny was in agreement with him. They decided that it was best if only Dumitru left and she stayed home with the girls. They reasoned that if Jeny came along and we were caught and thrown in jail, they would have no one to look after their kids. In preparation for our departure, Dumitru wrote a fake note to his wife, saying that he was sorry but he had decided to leave the country; he hadn't been able to tell her, but he loved her. He showed her the note and she said it was okay. He then put it in his Sunday suit. In about a week, when we would hopefully be in Yugoslavia, she could say that she had found the note. That way, the police wouldn't harass her.

We decided to leave in the beginning of May, hoping it wouldn't rain. We had studied the moon phases and planned our trip during a week with a new moon; that meant the sky would be dark. After all, we didn't want to be seen crossing the border. That same week, there was also a very important soccer game to be played and broadcasted on TV, and a lot of people would want to watch it.

John had obtained a visa for two months—April and May 1986. The first two times when he had come to Romania, we slept apart. I could see that he was determined to get me out and he had made every effort to have our family back together. In April, I accepted him as my husband; by the end of the month, I realized that I might be pregnant, but I didn't know for sure. I decided not to worry about it since there was nothing I could do.

On May 4, Easter Sunday in Romania, John and I went to church in the morning. In the afternoon, we went to the evening service at a church called Bethel.

Today is the day! I thought. *Lord, please help us.*

At 9:00 p.m., we took the train to Timisoara and arrived at 11:00 at night to meet with Dumitru and Florian. Watching closely to make sure nobody was after us, we snuck outside to the car that was waiting for us. A young friend of my cousins had volunteered to give us a ride. We needed to go to a little town called Eftimie Murgu, which was positioned at the foot of the mountains we wanted to cross. We didn't want to follow the road too close to the border, because we wanted to avoid police checkpoints; we wanted to travel without being suspected.

Close to town, there was a very renowned hot springs resort by the name of Baile Herculane—or Hercules' Baths. If asked by the police, we could say that we were going over there. If things didn't work out, we could claim we were coming from that resort and going home.

We were excited, singing songs of victory. It seemed like we were going just for the fun of it. It took us a good four-hour ride to get there. At about 3:00 in the morning, we got out of the car and said goodbye to the driver. Right there, by the streetlight,

John divided the luggage in three parts, one for each man. I protested and said that I could carry something, but John said, "No, you don't carry anything."

We noticed there were about three or four men talking and looking at us. John assumed they were coming off their shift in the nearby mine. We then had to climb a steep hill and some dogs started chasing us, so we crawled fast in the darkness to get away from them. By the time I got to the top, I was out of breath and really glad John hadn't let me carry anything. That was the first shock of the trip.

We had packed only what was strictly necessary for the trip—one sleeping bag, some blankets, warm clothes, food for about a week, and the boat. As we walked along, one of my cousins said, "John, I think your luggage is lighter than mine!" Right away, John replied, "Let's switch!" After a while, they would think the other one was lighter and switch again. John was willing to do anything and everything to accommodate the others.

After an hour of walking in the stillness of the forest, the bulb of the flashlight burned out. We had packed two batteries, which were hard to find, but we hadn't imagined that the new bulb would give out so soon. Maybe that was a blessing in disguise, because at night you could be seen more easily with a light on. John helped me step by step and held my hand all the way to the border! He was really glad that we were together. I remember that he held my left hand. It was dark, we could barely see, and it rained. With my right foot, I stepped into a slushy puddle and my foot got all soaked and muddy. I kept walking, and in a few hours my tennis shoe dried up and the mud shook off all on its own.

We had forgotten the map at home, but it wouldn't have helped us much anyway. There were no traffic signs in these old forests. We didn't follow any roads or paths; we just kept moving south, through valleys, over mountains, and across rivers and steep rocks. Our only guide was God and the compass, and that was enough. We knew that if we continued south, we would reach the Danube in four or five days. Many people tried going this way and some of them ended up lost for a month in the forest, out of food. I wasn't used to so much walking, but we had to keep going. We didn't run; we just kept up a steady pace. We didn't feel chased or followed by anybody. We weren't fugitives but hikers on a long trip.

Around 7:00 a.m., after four hours of walking, we stopped to eat and rest until noon. Then we hit the road again. Every time we stopped, John took off my shoes and massaged my feet. We were in good spirits. We had never been here before, but the compass kept us on track. We would set a target due south and then try to reach it. The target could be a cliff, a tree, or some other spot. We could only walk during the day. There were no villages or houses, only mountains, forests, rocks, and rivers to cross.

Once, we heard sheep in the distance and saw some shepherds. I don't think they saw us, but their dogs barked furiously and tried to chase us away. We had some walking sticks to help us climb and keep away dogs or other wild animals. If there were some random dwellings, we went out of our way to avoid them. Residents in that area were instructed to report to the police every stranger they saw. We knew that and didn't want to be seen. We walked from sunrise to sunset.

We kept walking through forests of hardwood like hornbeam (Carpinus) and beech wood (Fagus). We enjoyed God's nature; there were many beautiful flowers, crystal clear brooks of water, and splendid weather. At one point, we came to a clearing that took our breath away with its beauty. Between the hills was a large funnel-shaped depression covered in wild garlic flowers. It truly was a sight to see!

Later on, we stopped again to eat and rest. John took off my shoes and massaged my feet. By now our muscles were really tight, like guitar strings. Walking tens of kilometres a day and climbing over difficult terrain, our muscles were strained to the max. After five minutes of rest, our muscles didn't want to stretch again for the long road. Once you sat down, it was hard to get up again—but we had to keep going, so we got up and walked deep into the forest.

Evening was fast approaching and we stopped for the night. There were only trees around us. We built a fire to keep away wild animals like wolves, bears, hogs, and snakes. For food, we had cold meat, canned fish, bread, and apples. We made some tea that first night. John had hung all the luggage in the trees or else the mice would've eaten our food.

All three men lay down side by side and they placed me in a sleeping bag by their heads. As tired as I was, I couldn't sleep. I was afraid that some bear might come and grab the sleeping bag with me in it. I told them that and then I slept between John and Dumitru. John put his hand over me.

It was both peaceful and scary to sleep in the forest. The night felt eerie; the whole time, I heard the unceasing *shhhhhh* of mice and other creatures crawling over and under a thick layer of dry leaves. There was also an owl watching the fire with big, round, surprised eyes, going *hoooooo-hoooooo* all night long. It changed its position from north to south to west to east, probably wondering what that mysterious thing was so bright and hot. We kept the fire burning until morning. The rustle around us never ceased, but we were too tired and we soon fell sound asleep.

The next morning, we got up feeling rested and ready for a new day. We ate, put out the fire, and then kept going. It was difficult climbing up and slipping down a thick layer of dry leaves or sandy ground. Coming down from the top onto sandy soil was more difficult than you can imagine. You put your foot down and it slipped out from under you. John taught me to sit on my bum and just slide down. I did that and I slid a long way until I ended up hitting a tree. It was fun, just like sliding down on a snowy slope when I was a kid. It worked a lot better than taking one step at the time.

Many times, on the top of the mountain, we were tired and thirsty but had run out of water. We had to cross a few rivers with our shoes in our hands. The icy water burned our bare feet and froze our hearts. By the time I'd get to the other side, I felt like I had one frozen heart and two stumps instead of feet. We passed through a very young forest with thin trees. And look! There was somebody's lunch bag, a little cloth pouch hanging from a tree. How long had it been there? Was somebody nearby? We had no idea.

Some mountains had no trees on them; they were just steep and bare. I got dizzy looking down. We had to cross a few roads, so we made sure no lonely car or truck passed by. Once Dumitru got down on a road and signalled with his hand for us to come down. As soon as we were on the road, we heard and saw, to our horror, a police truck coming around the bend. Quick as lightning, we jumped off the road, not knowing how far down we had to go.

We went about two or three metres down. When I looked, I found myself riding a tree which had grown a little bent. Otherwise we were okay. That was a close call, because that vehicle had been transporting inmates to work in a forest or mine. The driver could have seen the dust on the road as we jumped off it.

After we ate, I begged John to make a fire because I longed for a hot drink. He did so, but then he thought he heard some noises and felt that the smoke was too thick. Not wanting to betray us, he put out the fire before we could make coffee or tea. Oh, how I missed a hot cup of tea or coffee! He didn't want us to be caught and risk everything.

On our way, we climbed from the top of one mountain to the top of another. On and on and on. There were mountains ahead of us and mountains behind us.

How much further must we walk? I asked myself.

At one point in our trip, I felt really sick. I felt weak and dizzy and became pale. I sat down, drank some water, and rested. Most likely I was just exhausted by our adventure. Thank God I recovered quickly and was soon ready to go again.

Are
WE THERE YET?

21

After hiking for hours and hours and hours, I felt lost between earth and sky. I saw mountains in the front, mountains in the back, mountains everywhere and wondered how much further I had to go. I got discouraged and longed to see the end of the tunnel. The luggage wasn't getting any lighter, either, except the bag with food. John was going to do something about that. He sat down and decided to sort through it. Did we need this? Did we need that? There wasn't much he could discard except Dumitru's toothpaste and brush. He threw them away, though many times after that Dumitru regretted it.

In a bright and sunny spot, we stopped by a small creek. I told John that I wanted to wash myself. I felt so dirty and dusty.

I went up the creek a few meters and hid behind a bush to wash myself. John was watching so nobody would surprise me. The water felt so refreshing! It was soft, as if it had soap in it. I felt revived afterwards.

Walking through the forests, we saw some wildlife. A small bear cub, followed by his mama, passed not far from us. Later on, a large hog crossed our way and disappeared into the forest. It had a really long snout and was as tall as a calf. Luckily, it didn't attack us; they could eat you alive, but thank God we were safe. A lot of snakes were coiled up, warming themselves in the sunshine. We thanked God it didn't rain at all. The weather was wonderful.

When the second night approached, we found ourselves at the top of a mountain. From there, we could see very far in the distance—the Danube! It looked like a narrow ribbon winding through the mountains. We were joyous. Not only were we on the right track, we could see the end of our journey—at least, on the Romanian side.

We didn't dare light a fire after that. What if soldiers or shepherds were in the area? To protect ourselves as best we could from wildlife during the night, we put tree branches and sticks in a circle around our sleeping area. Our hope was renewed.

On Wednesday, we continued our journey. Coming down from the mountain, we saw a lot of fallen logs. They were dry and clear of branches, making them easy to climb on; it was easier to walk on them than on the ground. I remembered my dream! I was on the right road. Some of the logs had names and dates carved on them; so and so had passed by here on such and such date. Other people had been here ahead of us.

We kept going. We had to climb another hill where there was a lot of brush, but we could see a nice clearing near the top with no bushes, just short grass. We could hardly wait to

get there. We had nearly reached it when we saw the house…
and the large dogs coming at us. We had to back down in the
brush.

We crossed another road and heard a truck coming up fast.
In a flash, we climbed up a steep slope covered in brush and
bushes. We barely made it up, but thank God we were safe. We
kept going and soon made it to the top of another hill.

John climbed a tree as agile as a monkey. "We're getting
closer," he called down. "I can see the river, and it's a lot bigger
now."

Dumitru wanted to see, too. He got up high in a tree, but
then fell down. At first, we were afraid he had broken a limb.
He was okay; only his dignity was hurt and his shoulder had a
bruise. Thank God he was in one piece.

We could hear more voices in the area. A larger creek flowed
toward the Danube nearby, and alongside it was a road. That
meant more people—cars and trucks. We thought it would be
wise to stay away from that valley. Being on the hill, we had
better visibility and could hide. There was no other flat terrain
around, only steep hills.

On that third night, we slept on a road that crossed the side
of a hill so steep that we would've rolled down quite easily if we'd
tried lying down on it. We couldn't make any fire and didn't put
branches around us like we had before. Very quietly, we lay down
to sleep. We were getting close. It was both exciting and scary.

The next day, we descended the hill and continued walking.
In about two hours, we saw a large area full of trees and bushes
that sloped down towards the Danube. From up high, we could
see the river in all its grandeur. It was very powerful—about a
mile wide—but the waves were so small that it seemed like it
was flowing upstream. We had to ask each other, "Which way
does it go?"

This body of water had claimed many lives. A lot of people had tried to cross it in search of freedom only to drown in the strong underwater currents. Looking at the water, I shivered. Could I cross this huge river safely? Could I make it to the other side, considering that I couldn't swim at all? Had it been worth the struggle to get here?

Yet, looking at this huge amount of water flowing south, I knew I was on the right track. I knew there was a God who had led me here, just like he had led my husband to come back to me. And I knew that just as I couldn't push back the Danube and have it flow north, I couldn't oppose the will of God, which meant that I should deeply and wholeheartedly reconcile with my husband. I knew I would be safe. With all the danger around me, with soldiers and rifles, residents and dogs, a humongous river and a tiny little boat, I knew I would be safe. Someone was watching over me.

Dumitru told us about other people who had tried to cross over to the Serbians. A dentist and his friend had been caught; when the soldiers heard that he was a dentist, they knocked the teeth out of his mouth in sick irony: "If he's a dentist, he can put them back!" When people tried to cross the Danube with boats or inflated mattresses, the guards weren't allowed to shoot towards the Serbian side; a bullet could go anywhere and kill an innocent civilian. But they did the next best thing: with a powerful motorboat, they would run over the poor escapees on their flimsy little boats until they had drowned and sunk to the bottom.

It was about 11:00 in the morning. The vegetation was very dense. We had to wait for nightfall to finally cross the river, because there were guards supposedly patrolling the area and we didn't want to be seen. We were maybe two hundred metres from the water and couldn't see any sentinels or checkpoints.

We got the boat out. It smelt brand new and it had some blue lines on it, but for the most part it was white—a dazzling white. We didn't want the white of the boat to glow in the dark and attract people, so we decided to smear it with black shoe polish.

While Florian helped me smear the boat, John and Dumitru decided to take a look around very carefully. They wanted to see how we could get to the water, where the soldiers' post was located, and gather any other useful information. They were gone for quite a while and we started to wonder what had happened.

More than two hours later, they made it back. John was ready to pull out his hair! They told us that they had gotten lost. Being in a new and strange place, with lush and abundant vegetation, they hadn't been able to find their way back at first. We were thankful to God that they had made it back safe and sound. Now we had to wait for nightfall.

They told us that trees, shrubs, and reeds grew right to the edge of the water. There wasn't a dry spot close by. It was only further down that they had found a tiny spot like a beach that was full of rocks and sand. Tonight we would have to go over there to inflate the boat and launch it. We had all our documents tied up and wrapped in plastic and Dumitru attached it to a string around his neck. We would only take the foreign currency from John when we got in the boat. I got ready to say goodbye to Florian and thanked him for coming along and helping us.

After ten o'clock, we had our last meal together—some salami, and the last two apples we split in two, so we each had half. It was really pitch dark outside; there was no moon, just like we'd wanted. We stood up and got ready to go.

Suddenly, two dogs came up to us, probably attracted by the smell of salami. They barked furiously! We couldn't defend ourselves. The deep, mad growling sent shivers down my spine. One was the size of a beast; I could feel its breath, its sharp teeth so close to me I could touch them. I feared they would rip us to pieces… and they seemed very determined to do so.

We froze. We couldn't move; we didn't dare. The dry leaves under our feet seemed to make a terrible noise. We started praying in despair. We were so close to freedom and yet so far. The slightest move made us feel like the whole universe was crumbling down around us. We were praying, praying, praying.

For half an hour, the dogs kept us still. We were becoming numb. Then, one by one, they left. The danger was still there, though. What if a soldier with a rifle was behind the dogs— or someone who lived in the area? For another ten or fifteen minutes, we didn't dare move. Then we took very finely ground black pepper and spread it around us. It's said that pepper goes up dogs' nostrils and keeps them away.

I then left with John and Dumitru, taking the boat to inflate and launch. Florian stayed behind. The two of them, but mostly John, inflated the boat just by blowing air into it with his mouth. Dumitru got into it first and sat facing the Romanian side of the river. I then kissed John, got in, and sat facing Yugoslavia.

Dumitru worked the oars after pushing off. The water was so still and calm that our boat was floating *up* the river, not down. It seemed like we were on a lake, not a rapidly flowing river. We went straight across. Once we were close to the Serbian side, we knew the soldiers couldn't touch us anymore.

"Go left, go right," I said periodically, guiding Dumitru. He had his back to the destination and couldn't see.

In about twenty minutes, we were by the other side. When we were closer, we noticed that the steep rock along the shore would be impossible to climb. We couldn't get off yet, so we sailed along. I could see here and there some sharp cliffs just poking out of the water, rocks which could damage our little boat. I told Dumitru to watch out for them. John had put one inflated plastic ring around my waist line, because he knew I couldn't swim. He had done that just in case something happened to the boat, so I could make it to the other side safely.

The sky was full of stars. The occasional splash of water came up into our little boat and soaked us. It had been about 1:00 in the morning when we got into the boat, and four hours later, by 5:00 a.m., we were able to get off. The river had flowed into a large and calm bay. Finally we were able to pull to the shore and get out. We pulled the plug to let the air out and then packed the boat as best we could, leaving it in some bushes.

We found a path which led us to the top of a gentle hill and started walking north. We were supposed to meet John in Beograd. Dumitru was so happy!

"Even the air seems cleaner here," he said. "Look where we came from! I'm so happy we got away and found freedom!"

Freedom

OR JAIL?

22

John watched the boat departing the Romanian shore. He stayed until he couldn't see it anymore, then turned to go back and find Florian. Suddenly, he froze! A soldier with a rifle wasn't far from him. John stood there, speechless. He didn't dare move. He squinted to see better. The soldier didn't move for five or ten minutes and John started to wonder whether it was a soldier or just the limb of a dry tree that looked amazingly similar. Slowly, very slowly, he started to move. The "soldier" didn't move. Whew! What a shock!

He found Florian and the two started back right away. They wanted to get as far away as possible from this very dangerous place. They walked almost continuously. The food was all gone, the boat was gone, and they only had the blankets and some extra jackets, which they decided to discard. They walked in two days what we had covered in more than three and a half days. They had blisters on the soles of their feet when they arrived home. On their way back, they found a shepherd's cottage and, being really tired, they decided to stop and rest a bit. When they walked in, everything was destroyed by a bear—and it seemed to have happened not long ago. They left in a hurry and kept on walking.

In the morning, they passed by a woman milking some cows. John talked to her and she gave them some milk. John drank about a litre. Florian didn't, because he knew it would give him the runs. Later on, they almost ran into a man cutting grass for silage with a scythe.

"What are you doing here?" he demanded.

"We're studying rocks," John told him. "We're scientists. Boy, you have a really nice place! I would love to live around here. Aren't you lucky to have such a nice place?"

The man approached with a pitchfork and they backed away. John kept talking. They moved on and avoided confrontation since they were headed away from the border.

John and Florian continued their trip, went to Resita, took the train, and returned home. It was Saturday night when John got back to my parents' house.

"Lidia is safe on the other side," he told them.

My mom had made cabbage rolls, which John loved. He ate, then went to bed. The next day, he took all my clothes, along with his luggage, and went to Beograd to find us.

My dad went with John to the train station. "Take care of my daughter. She is the weaker vessel."

John never forgot that charge.

On Friday morning, Dumitru realized that he had forgotten his nice leather jacket on the Danube's shore. Whoever had found it must have been very happy. I had also forgotten to take the money from John. It had been midnight, pitch dark, and we'd been trying to get away in a hurry. We had thought to take the money only when we were in the boat, as this would have been a criminal charge against us if we were caught. John realized our mistake right away and he tried to call us back, but we were too far. Plus, he didn't want to risk inviting the guards over.

We walked for about two hours before arriving at a bus station. Waiting for the bus were two older women dressed in traditional long skirts with scarves on their heads. As soon as they saw us, they started whispering to each other. We could only imagine what they said in their Serbian language: "Look at these two. They must be refugees. They must've crossed over that big river."

Very soon, a bus pulled up. We tried to tell the Serbian driver that we wanted to go to Beograd, but that we had no money. He was a kind-hearted man, and by his gestures we understood that he would give us a ride. We walked onto the bus and sat down on the left-hand side, near the back. We looked just like everyone else, except we kept quiet. The bus stopped two hours later in the centre of a community. People were getting on and off the bus, speaking loudly and laughing. Then one officer walked in and came straight to us.

"Documenti," he said.

Someone had reported us. I felt like the ground had split under my feet. My face turned deep red as everybody's eyes turned on us. We were the offenders and we had been caught.

We went to his office. He brought in a translator, because we didn't speak the same language. Even though we were the perpetrators, they treated us very well. They brought us a hot meal—steaming coffee, fried chicken, potatoes, and bread that was whiter and fresher than any I'd seen in a long time.

We were taken to another office and interrogated individually. The men here asked a lot of questions. We were refugees and they wanted to know why we had left Romania. They also checked our records to see if we were criminals or wanted for something. In order to find out, they had to ask about us in Romania. While waiting for the answer, they put us in jail for having crossed the border illegally. There was no legal way to cross the border.

Our outlook was quite grim. I was divorced, Dumitru had left his wife and two daughters at home, we didn't have the same last name, my mom and his dad were siblings, and we appeared suspicious. It had happened before that a man would abandon his family and leave the country with another woman. Nevertheless, my story matched Dumitru's—and also later on what John told them. While in jail, we lived with the fear that we would be sent back. We knew that eighty percent of escapees were sent back.

They took us to jail in a town called Pozarevac where they took all of our valuables—like watches and jewellery—until we were released. They put me alone in a room with three beds and a cubicle with a Turkish bathroom—a small room with nothing inside but a hole in the cement floor.

I was alone for five days, but I didn't mind. I used the time to think, to meditate, and on the fifth day John came to see me. I told him that I wanted some fruit, milk, and a small jar of honey. I had a big problem with haemorrhoids due to the fact that I hadn't eaten a hot meal during the week we had crossed the mountains. Another contributing factor was that the food in jail was extremely spicy. After eating the soup, the bottoms of the bowls were covered with black pepper. John brought me the requested items.

Then I had company, a young woman named Alana who had escaped from Romania by jumping off a ship and swimming to shore. She had almost drowned and couldn't drink water for a few days because she still had the sensation of drowning. Two old fishermen with a boat had come to her rescue. Alana was barefooted and also a chain smoker. She cried for cigarettes and got them every day.

I mentioned earlier that John and I had started sleeping together in April. It was in jail that I knew for certain that I was pregnant because I often threw up very heavily and felt nauseated. The smoke bothered me very badly. I threw up a few times daily, but Alana didn't care.

Another two women came in—a mother and her daughter, who turned eighteen in prison. The two of them slept in the third bed.

Once a week, we could have a hot shower. It felt so good. Once a day, the guards took us outside in the yard for half an hour. One of the guards was a very kind man. He saw me throwing up and offered me his chair, even though it meant he had to stand up. Some days I couldn't eat, so I would fast. Dumitru and other men would pass by my door and see the food left there.

"Tell your cousin to give us her food," the men told him. They had been working all day and could've eaten more.

After eighteen days, I was taken with Dumitru and two other men to Padinska Skela, a refugee camp north of Beograd. About one hundred fifty men were there, and one young woman named Stella. All of us were refugees from the surrounding countries. A tall, heavyset officer with light brown hair and thick, greasy lips (which he kept licking) took me to the room where Stella was staying. That night, this man came in ten times and asked if we needed tea, coffee, pills for headaches, or cookies.

"Forget about your husband," he said to me. "Don't go to Canada. Stay in Yugoslavia."

He promised he would come again.

The officers in that camp raped the women, even if their husbands were with them. They put husbands and wives in separate rooms, locked up the men, and went after the women. Dumitru had heard that they intended to put Stella and me in separate rooms the following night. By God's providence, John came to the camp the next day, paid a big pile of money as a bribe, and took me out. As soon as we were out the door, he put my bag down, took me in his arms, and turned me round and round and round until I was dizzy. I was the happiest girl in the world, and he was the happiest man. We were together and free!

When John had arrived in Yugoslavia, he had realized we were in jail. He then went to the police and found out where we were, and who the judge was in our case. The judge, seeing that all three of us were telling the truth, promised John that we would not be sent back. That was a great relief for all of us.

From the refugee camp, John took me to a motel. After that, we went to the Canadian Embassy in Beograd to ask for an entrance visa to Canada for me. I could see that John was well-known at the embassy, because one lady said to him, "Mister Pater, come here tomorrow at two o'clock. Not sooner than that, okay? Two o'clock, please." Apparently the Counsellor was in Greece on vacation and John had been begging his secretary to get in touch with him and help us. She did that and the Counsellor responded, giving me the Minister's Permit, a special kind of visa to come to Canada. All I needed was a medical check-up.

Being in a motel room, in a normal setting after more than three weeks of struggle and turmoil, I was able to finally relax and unwind. Our greatest worries were over. With God's help, we had succeeded in getting out of Romania, out of jail, and out of the refugee camp. We even had an assurance that I wouldn't be sent back. We slept well that night.

The next day, I called my mom. Right away, she said, "Where are you? What did you do? Why didn't you tell me?" She knew that the police was listening.

I caught on and said, "Mom, I'm really sorry. I left Romania with John, but I couldn't tell you that. I'm okay. We're in Beograd and I just got my visa to go to Canada. We're all set. I just need to do a medical check-up, then I'll call you from Canada. Mom, don't worry. John loves me very much. He's a good man and he takes good care of me. I love you, Mom. Say hi to Dad and to everybody."

My parents had been called to the police and harassed during my absence. "Where is your daughter?" they demanded.

"We don't know."

"What do you mean, you don't know?"

"We don't know! We have no idea. She's thirty-three years old and she didn't tell us anything."

They gave my parents a hard time, but they couldn't prove that my parents knew anything about my escape. The officers could see that my parents had nothing to hide. The little bird had flown away, but the police couldn't catch it.

It took thirty-two days for me to get from Romania to John's house in Canada. On May 9, we crossed the Danube into Yugoslavia, and on June 9, we flew to Canada. As far as I know, this is a record time for a refugee; it usually took at least three months. For other people, it could take years. I thank God for His care and protection.

GETTING *Ready*
TO COME HOME

23

When I went to the washroom the next morning, a blob the size of an egg dropped in the toilet bowl and I started bleeding right away. I called John, crying. "I think I had a miscarriage."

"Don't worry," he said. "You'll be okay."

We had to find a pharmacy and get some pads, then find a doctor for my medical check-up. We were in a foreign city, speaking a foreign language, and I was bleeding. In Romania, you couldn't buy pads.

After solving that problem, we found a lady doctor who saw me bleeding and sent me for an x-ray of the lungs to make sure I didn't have tuberculosis. The next day, I felt that something was wrong. Everything I ate tasted like ashes, or gravel. We bought some vanilla ice cream—it was so good, so creamy, so rich and smooth compared to the watery ice cream back home. Well, it tasted good on my tongue, but afterwards it was like sand.

I told John that we had to go back to the doctor. "Something is wrong and I don't know what."

We found the same lady and, after checking me up, she said, "You're pregnant." Then she wrote on a piece of paper that I was okay and that I was fit to fly on an airplane.

I pushed the paper aside. "I don't need that. It's me, and I don't feel good!"

Then she realized that the x-ray had killed the baby, so she sent me to have an abortion. The people at the abortion clinic put me to sleep while they performed the procedure. I felt better afterwards and I didn't have that same bad taste in my mouth.

I don't blame that doctor; we couldn't communicate properly and I had been bleeding. In a normal pregnancy, a woman wasn't supposed to bleed. Was it the stress of all that walking over the mountains, through icy rivers, and sleeping under the stars? Was it the sense of danger we went through? I had gotten my husband back and I would've loved to have a baby. I was thirty-three, John was thirty-nine, and we wanted to have a family.

My brother Avram lived in Koln, West Germany, with his wife Aurica and lovely daughter Gloria. They even had another beautiful daughter on the way! Little Annerose was born two weeks after I got to Canada. I hadn't seen my brother in five years, and the rest of his family in three years. I wanted to see them before we crossed the ocean. John talked to an agent from a travel agency. Being a refugee accepted by Canada, I should've flown straight to Calgary, but the travel agent understood my request. He gave us tickets from Beograd to Calgary with one overnight stop in Frankfurt.

From 3:00 p.m. on Sunday until 10:00 a.m. on Monday, we visited my relatives in Koln, and it was great. John had bought a return ticket for me because it was three hundred dollars cheaper than the one-way ticket. When we got to Canada, John saw me throw the return ticket in the garbage. He was very pleased. I didn't realize that I could've at least teased him for a month.

We left Frankfurt on Monday, June 9, 1986, at 10:00 a.m., flew nine hours, and arrived in Calgary at 11:00 a.m. the same day. It was the longest day of my life. People from the airplane clapped when we were five minutes to Calgary. Silently and secretly, I wiped away a few tears. How would my life be in this new country?

MY *Life* IN CANADA

24

Geno, a Romanian friend, picked us up from the Calgary airport and took us home to Lethbridge, a two-hour ride. John showed me our house. It was small and cute—and all paid for. He had told Phillip and Emma, good friends of his (and mine later on), "I'm going to Romania to pick up Lidia and I'm not coming back without her, even if I have to carry her on my back!" He just about had been forced to do that!

John and Phillip had been working together in road construction since John had come to Canada. Phillip later reminded us that when John was mad at work, he used to say, "I'll smash your 'front head,'" instead of forehead. John knew only two words in English when he first came to Canada: "Nice weather!"

On Wednesday, June 11, we got married by a lawyer in town. I met some wonderful Romanian people who attended our celebration. Actually, the husband was the first guy I had ever spoken with in Canada, the one I had told that John was dead to me, that I didn't want him to ever call me.

I was amazed at how friendly people were in this part of the world. Neighbours, people in the store, the bank, the church, the school… anywhere… when they heard I was new, they all said, "Welcome to Canada!" I felt very welcome. People were relaxed and peaceful. It was a very calm lifestyle.

The problems I'd had in Yugoslavia with the pregnancy didn't end after the abortion. For the next three weeks, I continued to bleed, but it was like blood from an infected wound. I told John that I needed to see a doctor, a gynaecologist. When the doctor consulted me, I felt an excruciating pain. He put me on very strong antibiotics for five days. I wasn't much better after that, so he had to perform surgery. A few days later, he told me that my uterus was broken; I had an open wound and a lot of blood inside. He told me that I could've died. He had cauterized my wound and cleaned me up really good inside.

When I heard him say "broken uterus" and "could've died," I remembered Maria, John's sister. She'd had a girl and a boy and was six months pregnant when I reconnected with them. All of a sudden, she felt really sick and went to the hospital. The doctors consulted her and didn't know what was wrong. If a pregnant woman tried to do something to terminate her pregnancy, the order from Bucharest was that she should be left to die. The doctors weren't supposed to help her if she had less than four children. Cases like that had happened and women had died. In Maria's case, the doctors debated what to do, choosing to operate on her. They told her, "You are a living miracle. Go and light up candles in every church in town and give thanks to God, because you were supposed to be dead. Your uterus was broken and the baby had fallen inside you and died." Luckily, she recovered and was okay.

"I have a boy and a girl," Maria had said to me. "I have a husband and we love each other. I would have welcomed another baby. If I wanted to do something to get rid of the baby, I wouldn't have waited until I was six months along. But I didn't do anything!"

Maria and I were the same age, both young and healthy, and there was a striking similarity in our cases. Could it be that somebody had tried to do something to harm us? I don't want to attribute any more power to the devil than he has, but for several weeks in a row I had found bags filled with garbage in front of my parents' house. The neighbours had said that they hadn't put them there. I took them in the yard and burned them. After I left Romania, there were no more garbage bags by the house.

I adjusted really well to life in Canada. I cannot say that everything was smooth in our lives, but we tried to work out every problem we had. I told John that I felt really slow and clumsy and I thought I should change. His advice? "Be who you are!" Right away, he put me at ease and I felt comfortable with who I was.

I had several dreams that made me believe that somebody was trying to destroy our family. In one, I had a small box and I had to walk past a window. The person on the other side of the window would then do something to make the box explode. I saw several boxes go to pieces in front of my eyes. But my box didn't explode; it just smoked on the inside.

In another dream, I had maybe thirty magnetic rings equal in size and shape. Together, they formed a tall bar. Each ring was almost as thick as a hockey puck, with a hole in the centre.

The bar was twenty-five centimetres tall, but somebody was trying to break the magnetic force of the rings and pull them apart. There were two or three rings sticking out on one side, and another two or three on the other, but the bar was not broken.

It also happened that both John and I felt a tremendous pressure on our shoulders. I felt like five hundred pounds were pushing down on me. This wasn't a dream; it was almost physical. In response, we both fasted three days in a row. I really think that the devil was trying his best to destroy us, but the power of God protected us.

John took me to a few churches in Lethbridge to see where we should attend. We were also looking for a sponsor for Dumitru, who was still in Yugoslavia. I couldn't sponsor him because I wasn't a Canadian citizen yet, and John couldn't because he wasn't a relative. Pastor Elmer Martin from the Pentecostal Assemblies on the west side of town offered to sponsor him right away. This was also the church where our friends Mike and Alice Putici attended. I really wanted to see them again and I knew they would be happy that I was here with John.

Pastor Martin had very clear diction, which helped me learn English. I started my life in Canada knowing just thirteen English words—peace, love, and joy… and I could count to ten. All the people in the church were very welcoming. I felt like family.

Dumitru came to Canada four months later, in October 1986. Two weeks after, I gave my testimony in church and Keith Newman, a good friend of ours, recorded it on videotape. I was badly murdering the English language trying to tell my life story, but the people were very kind.

It took three years for Dumitru's family to follow him to Canada. They came on April 12, 1989, after a lot of red tape, which was the norm for anybody trying to leave Romania legally.

They had no Easter holiday that year, because in Romania the holiday occurred later in April and in Canada it had passed by the time they arrived.

I went to college and took an English as a Second Language program. The teachers were very good. I remember Judy Hasinoff and how encouraging she was while I struggled to tell my story.

Mary Ro wrote me a few letters; they were the highlight of my days. In one of the letters, each lady from the office wrote a few words, but Mary didn't. She just drew a picture of two eyes crying tears and a sad mouth blowing me a kiss. It meant more than a thousand words to me.

When I'd been working in the office with them, the girls had jokingly expressed their doubts with regards to my relationship with Petrisor.

"You can say that you didn't sleep with him," one said, "but he's dead and you can say whatever you want now."

They didn't believe me! What hurt me the most was that Mary, my best friend, thought the same thing. She didn't know if she should believe me!

"Yes, he's dead," I told her, "and I can't prove to you that I didn't sleep with him, but there is a God in heaven, and He can do the impossible. May He prove it to you."

Mary had a dream that she went to her village, and there was Petrisor! Even though he had been dead for one and a half years, he was out in the street and wanted to talk to her. He asked her, "What do you know about Lidia?"

"I know that she's in Canada and she's happy. That's the way it was supposed to be. And anyhow, there was no intimate relationship between the two of you."

He agreed and emphasized these words: "That is true." Then he added, "When you send her a letter, write under the stamp 'I love you' from me." Mary wrote to me about all these things and that finally she believed I hadn't slept with him.

Mary also told me about the pastor from my church, Ioan Trutza, who had advised me not to go back to John. "If you knew how many times he talks about you in church, you wouldn't believe it! He doesn't give your name, but he's very impressed with you and how things turned out."

For two years, John and I tried to have family and couldn't. We were depressed. I envied every pregnant woman I saw. Every month I went to the doctor, kept charts, and was poked and prodded at, but it all seemed useless. The doctor operated on me a second time in 1988 and told me that my tubes were very badly infected; they were one-third the normal thickness. He said that if I didn't get pregnant within six months, I should try for a test-tube baby. John had tests done on him, too, and he was okay. Before I went to the hospital, I dreamed that Mary took a measuring tape and, with some scissors, wanted to cut off ten centimetres, but then she only cut six. The doctor told me that I would be in the hospital for ten days, but I was out in six.

I kept going to college, because I couldn't have kids. In 1988, I went for upgrading, and then in 1989 I registered for a Business Administration program at the same college. In late January 1989, I dreamed that somebody gave me two measuring tapes—each of them 150 centimetres long. I couldn't figure out what that meant! From my earlier dream, I knew that six centimetres meant six days of suffering—at least for me—and I figured out that there were about three hundred days of some trouble, or suffering, of some kind ahead.

I tried to discuss this dream with somebody, but this person said, "Oh, the prophetess Lidia! She's telling us her dreams!"

I felt hurt. *You mock me now*, I thought, *but never again will I tell you anything.*

Where was my Mary? I had been able to tell her anything and she had never made fun of me.

By December 1989, after the Revolution in Romania, I understood that it had meant three hundred more days of communism for Romania.

Recently, I heard the testimony of a former officer in the Romanian Securitate. He talked about how he had tortured and killed Christians while on duty. He was once tipped about eighteen people who were trying to escape, and the point of their crossing. He was ready and waiting for them—but they didn't come. A bunch of farmers, hoes on their shoulders, showed up and started to hoe the rows of corn. They even greeted him from under their large-brimmed hats, waving goodbye to him. When they reached the end of their rows, they dropped their hoes and crossed over to the other side! They had been the ones!

When he reported the story to his superior, he was furious! "Catch the one who guided them!" his boss ordered.

They found the guide and emptied thirty-six bullets in him. About fifteen years later, when this officer shared his testimony in church, a man told him that he had been that guide! Somehow, all those bullets had passed through his stomach and he'd survived. A group of farmers had found him after the soldiers left and took him to a hospital.

Another two years passed, and I felt that I was pregnant again. John and I were ecstatic. The doctor said, "Fantastic, unbelievable, incredible!"

"Why are you so happy?" I asked.

"With the type of surgeries you had, only one in seven women gets pregnant. I guess you are the seventh!"

Later on, the doctor offered John the stethoscope to listen to the baby's heartbeat. I listened, too. The heart went *tick-tick, tick-tick, tick-tick* like a bubbly brook. John still couldn't believe it and said, "Isn't that Lidia's heart?" Then the doctor put the stethoscope on my heart, which was beating at a much lower pitch—*tam-tam tam-tam tam-tam*, just as booming and deep as the Danube.

We had a beautiful baby boy and named him Samuel. Two years later, we had a beautiful baby girl who we named Becky, short for Rebecca.

When our daughter was nine months old, I had a third surgery, a complete hysterectomy. The doctor told me that I had such a terrible mess inside again that he had to take it all out. That same day in Romania, our brother-in-law Traian, Maria's husband, died. He had only been forty years old but very overweight.

John and I became very good friends with another couple, about our age, Ron and Dorothy Babin. Ron's mother, Susan, was at odds with Dorothy. One Friday morning, I called Dorothy at the bank where she worked and said, "I know it's Friday and you're very busy, but allow me one minute. I dreamed that Ron's mom had ten snakes—some small, some very big—and she decided to kill them all. I think it means your relationship is going to improve." That evening, Susan's sister from California invited all three of them to go for a vacation.

"I remembered your dream and decided to give it a try," Dorothy later told me. They went and had such a good time that the following year Dorothy and Susan travelled back to California together—this time, just the two of them. It changed their relationship for the better.

When I was in college in 1990, John took a class as well, updating his license as an automotive mechanic. We met for lunch in the cafeteria everyday. One of his classmates was Peter VanLiere, a tall and young Dutch man who was also a mechanic and joined us for lunch daily. I noticed that Peter always prayed for his lunch, then retrieved a New Testament from his front pocket after he ate and read a few verses.

"Let's marry him to Camelia," I told John, impressed by Peter. Camelia was my brother's daughter from Romania. Camelia also had a sister, Simona, who was a year younger.

"They're half a world apart," John reminded me. "He doesn't speak Romanian and she doesn't speak English!"

It took a while, but they got in touch. Peter wanted to go to Holland for his cousin's wedding and also to see Camelia. I asked her if she wanted me to buy some fabric for her dress if she decided to marry him.

"You sew the dress for me!" she suggested. I had sewed some outfits for Camelia and her sister Simona when they were young.

I started sewing her dress. My son was two years old and wanted to sit on my lap every time I used the sewing machine, and at the time I was pregnant with my daughter. Peter's mom acted as our seamstress and helped me with the dress. She did most of the work and was delighted to help. She tried it on Peter, since his measurements were the same as Camelia's.

Peter had a beard and was wearing his bride's dress!

Peter went to Holland and then to Romania with the dress in his suitcase. The two had never met before, but they got married in Romania and six months later came to Canada. They have five children now and are our neighbours. Camelia's sister used the same dress in Romania when she got married.

We moved to a farm when our kids were young, and they were bussed to school every day. Becky was a tomboy, a true farm girl. She had long, blond hair and never wanted to move to town. We planted a lot of trees on our farm and Sam and Becky watered them. It had been a bare prairie field when we moved onto our land. There hadn't even been a house on it.

We were offered a house that was located in town and had to be demolished. We took it. The movers brought it in, but we had to renovate everything inside. John was a very handy man, and very focused. I wanted to be close by, so we could help finish the house.

While the house was getting ready, I decided that we should move into the quonset, a large corrugated tin building that farmers use to store their machinery over winter. We lived there for a month without water or bathroom facilities. About five days after we moved in, a former neighbour, a sweet and petite lady named Julie Stiles, brought us supper out of the goodness of her heart. Her two boys, Nicholas and Nathaniel, were about same age as our kids and they had fun with the old machinery on our farm.

Half an hour after Julie's visit, another friend, Dan Speakman, came by and said, "We have a promotion at work, so I brought you this twenty-litre water jug and the frame that comes with it. You can use it for a month with no obligation." As soon as he left, our lawyer, Steve Denecky, came by: "I called your phone number for five days; I have a cheque in your name for $22,000. Here it is!" The cheque was for the balance between what we had paid for the farm and the final cost.

That day is set in my mind as the day of God's blessing, provision, and protection for our family. Within two hours, we got the food, the water, and the money—all in the right order. It was a good omen and I knew we would be fine. I had a very good feeling about our farm.

We didn't have a phone for a month, and after that the phone line was on the ground for a whole year. The dog used to chew up the line and we didn't have a ringtone. We had to go find the broken wire and patch the line so we could talk on the phone. The line is now buried.

I once spoke to a mother who told me that there had been a lice outbreak at school and her daughter came home with lice. I was shocked! I didn't think that this could happen in Canada, only in poor countries. I told her to put her child in the bathtub, let her hair loose, then soak it really good with rubbing alcohol for five minutes from the scalp of her head to the very tip of her hair. It was safe and sanitary and would clear the lice. Some of the things I knew from Romania came in handy even in Canada!

Another example of God's protection for our family stands out very clearly in my mind. We knew a family that had moved from Romania to Canada in August 1999, because they wanted a better life for their children. Their son, Mike, became good friends with our son, Sam, and their daughter Roxana was very fond of Becky. The father had once been a university professor in Romania and his wife had been an executive with a smaller company. They were hard-working and determined to succeed.

On August 26, 2001, Mike turned fifteen and he invited our kids to his birthday party. His mother, her two children, and two other boys in the van were on their way to our house to pick up our kids. Unfortunately, they never made it. Less than two minutes from our house, she missed a stop sign and they were hit full-force by a truck and trailer hauling thirty-six tons of gravel. In an instant, all five people in the van were killed, along with the truck driver. It was a great tragedy that shook our town, and in all that I felt God's protective hand right around us.

We felt heartbroken for the terrible loss and prayed for all the families that had suffered such a great tragedy. This husband and father was left alone. He missed his wife and kids terribly and a year later he shot himself.

There are twists and turns in our lives that we could never foresee.

One day, about three years ago, Sam our son, now a University student said, "Mom guess what? I met a Romanian in school today! [There are not very many Romanians in our area.] As I was passing by in a hall way, I heard this man reply 'Poftim?' which is Romanian for 'Pardon me?' Right away I asked him 'Are you Romanian?'"

The man confirmed that he was indeed. He also told Sam that he is a University professor that had just moved to Lethbridge from Hamilton.

"And Mom, I invited him to come to our place for lunch on Sunday!"

"What?" I replied.

"Well Mom, you always invite people, so I did too."

On Sunday we met this gentleman and his mother, a lovely lady named Lidia Ghioca. Her son, Dragos Ghioca, the University professor, is a brilliant mathematician, so much so, that he has a theorem by his name. His mother told us that in 1997 and 1998 he participated in Putnam competition with other 2500 University students from USA and Canada and he placed 30th. The following year he was on the tenth place of the 2500. Dragos is recognized internationally as very energetic and a leader in the field of number theory. I am very proud of Dragos and his mother and for the exceptional example that he is. Thank God.

Was

IT WORTH IT?

25

Yes, a hundred times yes.

Sometimes we wonder, *What if?* What would've happened if we wouldn't have separated, or if Petrisor wouldn't have died or we wouldn't have escaped? What would have happened then? Only God knows. John is aware of the fact that when he came to reconcile with me, that's when he finally broke away from his sinful past. Also, he doesn't drink hard liquor anymore.

I can say that I have no regrets for what happened in our past. God has been so great in restoring our relationship and our family... all glory goes to God. Also, I hold no grudges against anyone, not even Nona. She didn't do what she did because she hated me, but rather because she wanted John and I happened to be in the way. She is a soul who needs God's mercy and salvation, just like the rest of us.

John would express his gratitude and thankfulness to the Canadian authorities, who had all kept their word and helped us. Canada truly is a wonderful place to live and no one appreciates it more than John and me. The words of the authorities in the communist country, on the other hand, meant nothing.

John never really wanted to talk about his past life. "I went to Romania and brought my wife to Canada," he said. "That's as far back as I want to go about what happened in the past." One time he admitted to me, "When I went home and saw Nona, I would leave right away and go back to work. I was in road construction and was gone all the time. I'd had a golden egg and lost it. I hated being with Nona. It was a miserable life."

We attend First Baptist Church in Lethbridge, Alberta. Our pastor is Bruce Martin, a kind and gentle man. I was asked to lead a ladies' Bible study, but I felt very unqualified for this position. I decided that I would ask one of the other women from the group to lead it instead. I thought if someone else led the Bible study for a few weeks, I could then just tell her to continue since she did a better job of it than I could.

In my daily Bible reading, I was in the book of Ezekiel. One of the verses jumped off the page at me: *"Instead of carrying out your duty... you put others in charge..."* (Ezekiel 44:8). I felt convicted and knew that God wanted me to be there, so I stopped trying to pass the buck.

Rarely a day goes by that my husband doesn't tell me how much he loves me and how thankful he is to God for His kindness towards us. I love him, too, and I'm very thankful to God for our life. No one knows better than me how much John changed for the better. No man on this earth could love and appreciate me more than him, and I know that so well! That's why my heart aches when I see young people around us making so many wrong choices. I think about how much grief and sorrow they are causing, first of all to their own soul, and second to those around them. I pray to God with all my heart that they will turn around—the sooner the better.

All the glory goes to God.

If it had been up to me, I would have married Petrisor, but God intervened. Well, the truth is we aren't perfect, but we need to know where we once were and where we are now—in God's grace.

I know that our purpose on Earth is to glorify God. That's the reason God created us according to Isaiah 43:7. Our family has every reason to honour God. But so do you! Know that God loves you and wants the best for you. Just tell Him that you accept Him as your personal Saviour and He will set your life in the right direction.

Someone may question my dreams and say that it's just my imagination or the cabbage rolls from last night. Throughout history, there were many people who had dreams, and they knew with certainty that they meant something. Remember Joseph, Daniel, and Pharaoh? They had dreams that were very significant. Paul from the New Testament had a dream, too: "Come to Macedonia and help us." If you have a dream like that, it will move you. I would dare say that my life is proof that my dreams came from Him. They led me to a good place. I trust in God one hundred percent.

God didn't just speak to me through dreams, though. In December 2009, I received a popup card from a Salvation Army outlet for a donation. On it, I read a message from God to me: *He heals the brokenhearted and binds up their wounds* (Psalm 147:3)

God, that is me! I thought. *You, Lord, reminded me how broken my heart was and how many times. Now my heart is healed—and my wounds, too! Thank you, Lord!*

Our reconciliation is a miracle. Our children are just as much a miracle from God. They are now twenty-one and nineteen years old. We are so blessed. Praise God!

Canada is a blessed country and I feel at home here. I am at peace.

We know that the power of God restores and blesses our family. Out of the ashes, out of nothing, He made something beautiful. Glory to God!

Every time we talk about our story, someone says, "Why don't you write a book?" We have had a lot of requests over the years. Now, our kids tell our story and are asked whether or not we have a book. Many times my daughter tells me, "Mom, God gave you a story, but you need to write it down." It took a quarter of a century to do it, but here it is!

John and I recently celebrated twenty-six years in Canada, along with the twenty-sixth anniversary of our second marriage. We couldn't be more blessed.

Glory to God.